FR 96 £6.95

English Grammar for Students of French

The Study Guide for Those Learning French

Third edition

Jacqueline Morton

Hill Press®

ENGLISH GRAMMAR series

English Grammar for Students of Spanish
English Grammar for Students of German
English Grammar for Students of Italian
English Grammar for Students of Latin
English Grammar for Students of Russian
English Grammar for Students of Japanese
Gramática española para estudiantes de inglés

© 1993, Jacqueline Morton

Printed in the U.S.A.

Library of Congress Catalog Card Number: 87-7889

ISBN 0-934034-18-4

Contents

TO THE STUDENT

English Grammar for Students of French explains the grammatical terms that are in your French textbook and shows you how they relate to English grammar. Once you have understood the terms and concepts in your own language, it will be easier for you to undertand your textbook. With simple explanations and numerous examples this handbook compares English and French grammar, pointing out the similarities and differences.

Most teachers incorporate **English Grammar** into the class syllabus so you will know which pages to read before doing an assignment in your French textbook. If you are selecting the pages yourself, check the detailed index for the terms and concepts you will need to understand for your assignment. When you finish a chapter in the handbook, you can test your comprehension by doing the short Reviews and checking your answers against the Answer Key.

Tips for Studying a Foreign Language

1. RULES — Make sure you understand each rule before you move on to the next one. Language learning is like building a house; each brick is only as secure as its foundation.

2. MEMORIZATION — Memorization plays an important part in language learning. For instance, you will have to memorize vocabulary, verb conjugations, and grammar rules. To memorize, here are the steps you should follow:

   - Divide the passage into sections you can easily remember (for instance, 2 sentences or 5 words).
   - Read the first section aloud several times.
   - Write down the first section as you repeat it aloud to yourself.
   - Compare what you wrote with the original.
   - Repeat the above until there is no difference between what you said or wrote and the original.
   - Repeat these steps to memorize the second section.
   - Continue memorizing each section in the same way, reciting from the beginning each time.

3. VOCABULARY — Use any trick or gimmick that helps you remember new words. Here are some that students have found useful:

- Write each word on a separate index card, French on one side, English on the other.
- Use index cards or pens of different colors. This can help you remember other useful information about the word: using blue for masculine nouns and red for feminine nouns will help you remember genders. (You can also use green for verbs, orange for adjectives, etc. to remember parts of speech.)
- When learning the French words, look at the English words. Say the French word that corresponds aloud, and flip the card to check your answer. Shuffle the deck often so you see the English word cold (i.e., without remembering the word order).

4. WRITTEN EXERCISES — Read the French words and sentences out loud as you write them. That way you are practicing seeing, saying, and hearing the words. It will help you remember them.

5. DAILY PRACTICE — Don't get behind. It's almost impossible to catch up in language learning because you need daily practice and time to absorb the material.

6. LANGUAGE TAPES — It is better to listen to tapes for short periods several times during the week rather than doing everything in one long session.

Bonne chance,

Jacqueline Morton

INTRODUCTION

When you learn a foreign language, in this case French, you must look at each word in three ways:

1. The **meaning** of the word—An English word must be connected with a French word that has an equivalent meaning.

   Boy, a young male child, has the same meaning as the French word **garçon**.

Words with equivalent meanings are learned by memorizing vocabulary. Sometimes two words are the same or very similar in both English and French. These words are called **cognates** and are, of course, easy to learn.

French	English
intelligent	intelligent
gouvernement	government
continuer	continue

Occasionally knowing one French word will help you learn another.

Knowing that **étudiant** is a male student should help you learn that **étudiante** is a female student; or knowing that **vendeur** is a salesman should help you remember that **vendeuse** is a saleswoman.

Usually there is little similarity between words, and knowing one French word will not help you learn another. As a general rule, you must memorize each vocabulary item separately.

   Knowing that **garçon** is *boy* will not help you learn that **fille** is *girl*.

In addition, there are times when words in combination take on a special meaning.

   The French word **faire** means *to make*; **la queue** means *the tail*. However, **faire la queue** means *to line up, to stand in line*.

An expression whose meaning as a whole (**faire la queue**) is different from the meaning of the individual words (**faire** and la **queue**) is called an **idiom**. You will need to be aware of these idiomatic expressions in order to recognize them and use them correctly.

2. The **classification** of the word—English and French words are classified in eight categories called **parts of speech**. Here is a list of the

parts of speech:

noun	article
verb	adverb
pronoun	preposition
adjective	conjunction

Each part of speech has its own rules for spelling, pronunciation, and use. You must learn to identify the part of speech of each word in order to choose the correct French equivalent and to know what rules to apply.

Look at the word *what* in the following sentences:

a. *What* do you want?
b. *What* movie do you want to see?
c. I'll do *what* you want.[1]

The English word is the same in all three sentences; but in French three different words will be used and three different sets of rules will apply because each *what* belongs to a different part of speech.

3. The **use** of the word—A word must also be identified according to the role it plays in the sentence. Each word, whether English or French, plays a specific role. Determining this role or **function** will also help you to choose the correct French equivalent and to know what rules to apply. Here is a list of functions:

subject
direct object
indirect object
object of a preposition

Let us go back again to the word *what*.

a. *What* is on the table?
b. *What* is she doing?
c. *What* are you talking about?[2]

---

[1] a. Interrogative pronoun, see p. 138.
b. Interrogative adjective, see p. 101.
c. Relative pronoun without antecedent, see p. 166.

[2] a. Subject, see p. 28.
b. Direct object, see p. 116.
c. Object of a preposition, see p. 119.

The English word is the same in all three sentences; but in French three different words will be used because each what has a different function.

Careful

As a student of French you must learn to recognize both the part of speech and the function of each word in a given sentence. This is essential because words in a French sentence have a great deal of influence on one another.

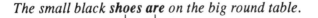

The small black shoes are on the big round table.

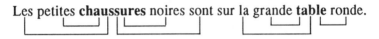

Les petites **chaussures** noires sont sur la grande **table** ronde.

IN ENGLISH

The only word that affects another word in the sentence is *shoes*, which forces us to say *are*. If the word were *shoe*, we would have to say *is*.

IN FRENCH

The word for *shoes* (**chaussures**) not only affects the word for *are* (**sont**), but also the spelling and pronunciation of the French words for *the, small*, and *black*. The word for *table* (**table**) affects the spelling and pronunciation of the French words for *the, big*, and *round*. The only word not affected by another word is **sur**, which means *on*.

Since parts of speech and function are usually determined in the same way in English and in French, this handbook will show you how to identify them in English. You will then learn to compare English and French constructions. This will give you a better understanding of the explanations in your French textbook.

1. WHAT IS A NOUN?

A **noun** is a word that can be the name of a person, an animal, place, thing, event, or an idea.

IN ENGLISH
Let us look at some different types of words which are nouns:

- a person
  professor, clown, student, girl
  Professor Smith, Bozo, Paul, Mary
- an animal
  dog, bird, bear, snake
  Heidi, Tweetie, Teddy
- a place
  city, state, country, continent
  Paris, Michigan, France, Europe
- a thing
  lamp, airplane, book, dress
  Perrier, Eiffel Tower, Arch of Triumph
- an event
  or activity
  graduation, marriage, birth, death, football
  robbery, rest, growth
- an idea
  or concept
  poverty, democracy, humor, mathematics
  addition, strength, elegance, virtue, increase

As you can see, a noun is not only a word which names something that is tangible, i.e., that you can touch, such as *table, dog*, and *White House*, it can also be the name of things that are abstract, i.e., that you cannot touch, such as *justice, jealousy*, and *honor*.

A noun that does not state the name of a specific person, place, thing, etc. is called a **common noun**. A common noun does not begin with a capital letter, unless it is the first word of a sentence. All the words above that are not capitalized are common nouns.

A noun that is the name of a specific person, place, thing, etc. is called a **proper noun**. A proper noun always begins with a capital letter. All the words above that are capitalized are proper nouns.

The girl is Mary.
common   proper
noun   noun

A noun that is made up of two words is called a **compound noun**. A compound noun can be a common noun, such as *comic strip* and *ice cream* or a proper noun, such as *Western Europe* and *North America*.

To help you learn to recognize nouns, look at the paragraph below where the nouns are in *italics*.

The best *purchases* from *France* include *wines, perfumes, scarves, gloves* and other luxury *items*. Today, French *workers* make excellent *skis* and *tennis rackets* which are sold the *world* over. Thanks to the *Common Market*, you can find *goods* from *Germany, Italy, England*, and their commercial *partners* in all large French *stores*. Thus, Italian *sportscars*, English *leather*, German *glassware*, and Belgian *lace* can be bought at *prices* comparable to those in the *country* of *origin*.

IN FRENCH
Nouns are identified in the same way as they are in English.

Terms Used to Talk About Nouns

GENDER – A noun has a gender; that is, it can be classified according to whether it is masculine, feminine, or neuter (see **What is Meant by Gender?**, p. 6).

NUMBER – A noun has a number; that is, it can be identified according to whether it is singular or plural (see **What is Meant by Number?**, p. 9).

COUNT OR NON-COUNT – A noun can be classified as to whether it is a count noun or non-count noun; that is, whether it refers to something that can be counted or not (see p. 15 in **What are Articles?**).

FUNCTION – A noun can have a variety of functions in a sentence; that is, it can be the subject of the sentence (see **What is a Subject?**, p. 28) or an object (see **What are Objects?**, p. 116).

▼▼▼▼▼▼▼▼▼▼▼▼▼▼REVIEW ▼▼▼▼▼▼▼▼▼▼▼▼▼▼▼▼

Circle the nouns in the following sentences:

1. The boy came into the classroom and spoke to the teacher.

2. The textbook has a painting on its cover.

3. Mary Evans visited Paris with her class.

4. The lion roared and the children screamed.

5. Truth is stranger than fiction.

6. His kindness and understanding were known throughout the world.

2. WHAT IS MEANT BY GENDER?

Gender in the grammatical sense means that a word can be classified as masculine, feminine, or neuter.

Gender is not very important in English; however, it is at the very heart of the French language where the gender of a word is often reflected in the way the word is spelled and pronounced. More parts of speech have a gender in French than in English. Parts of speech that indicate gender:

English	French
pronouns	nouns
possessive adjectives	articles
	pronouns
	adjectives

Since each part of speech follows its own rules to indicate gender, you will find gender discussed in the sections dealing with articles and the various types of pronouns and adjectives. In this section we shall only look at the gender of nouns.

IN ENGLISH

Nouns themselves do not have a gender, but sometimes their meaning will indicate a gender based on the biological sex of the person or animal the noun stands for. When we replace a proper or common noun with *he* or *she,* we automatically use *he* for males and *she* for females. All the nouns which name things that do not have a sex are replaced by *it.*

Nouns referring to males indicate the **masculine** gender.

> Paul came home; *he* was tired, and I was glad to see *him*.
> noun   masculine   masculine
> male

Nouns referring to females indicate the **feminine** gender.

> The girl came home; *she* was tired, and I was glad to see *her*.
> noun   feminine   feminine
> female

All other nouns which do not indicate a biological gender are considered **neuter.**

> The city of Washington is lovely. I enjoyed visiting *it*.
> noun   neuter

There are a few well-known exceptions, such as *ship,* which is referred to as *she.* It is custom, not logic, which decides.

The S/S United States sailed for Europe. *She* was a beautiful ship.

IN FRENCH

All nouns—common nouns and proper nouns—have a gender; they are either masculine or feminine. Do not confuse the grammatical terms "masculine" and "feminine" with the meaning of "male" and "female." Only a few French nouns have a grammatical gender tied to whether they refer to someone of the male or female sex, most nouns have a gender which must be memorized.

The gender of nouns based on **biological gender** is easy to determine.These are nouns whose meaning is always tied to one or the other of the biological sexes, male or female.

Males → masculine	Females → feminine
Paul	Mary
boy	girl
brother	sister
son	daughter

The gender of all other nouns, common and proper, cannot be explained or figured out. These nouns only have a **grammatical gender** which is unrelated to biological sex. Here are some examples of English nouns classified under the gender of their French equivalent.

Masculine	Feminine
boat	car
suicide	death
Japan	France
blackboard	chalk
government	democracy

Gender is important not only for the noun itself, but for the spelling and pronunciation of the words it influences. You will have to memorize the grammatical gender of every French noun you learn. Since a noun alone does not usually indicate its gender, when memorizing vocabulary you will have to learn a noun with its article because the article does indicates gender (see **What are Articles?**, p. 12).

Careful

You cannot rely on biological gender to indicate the gender of French equivalents of nouns such as *professor* which can refer to a female or male. Such nouns only have a grammatical gender which must be memorized.

▼▼▼▼▼▼▼▼▼▼▼▼▼▼REVIEW ▼▼▼▼▼▼▼▼▼▼▼▼▼▼▼▼

Circle M (masculine) or F (feminine) next to the nouns whose gender you can identify, and (?) next to the nouns whose gender you would have to look up in a dictionary.

GENDER IN FRENCH

1. boys	M	F	?
2. chair	M	F	?
3. Jane	M	F	?
4. classroom	M	F	?
5. visitor	M	F	?
6. sisters	M	F	?
7. houses	M	F	?

3. WHAT IS MEANT BY NUMBER?

Number in the grammatical sense means that a word is singular or plural. When a word refers to one person or thing, it is said to be **singular**; when it refers to more than one, it is **plural**.

More parts of speech indicate number in French, and there are more spelling and pronunciation changes in French than in English. Parts of speech that indicate number:

English	French
nouns	nouns
verbs	articles
pronouns	verbs
only demonstrative	pronouns
adjectives	adjectives

Since each part of speech follows its own rules to indicate number, you will find number discussed in the sections dealing with articles, the various types of adjectives and pronouns, as well as in all the sections on verbs and their tenses. In this section we shall only look at the number of nouns.

IN ENGLISH

A singular noun is made plural in one of two ways:

1. A singular noun can add an *"-s"* or *"-es"*.

book	books
kiss	kisses

2. A singular noun can change its spelling.

man	men
mouse	mice
leaf	leaves
child	children

A plural noun is usually spelled and pronounced differently from the singular.

Some nouns, called **collective nouns,** refer to a group of persons or things, but the noun itself is considered singular.

A football *team* has eleven players.
The *family* is well.
The *crowd* was under control.

IN FRENCH

As in English, the plural form of a noun is usually spelled differently from the singular. The most common change is the same as the one made in English; that is, an **"-s"** is added to the singular noun.

livre	livres	*book*	*books*
table	tables	*table*	*tables*

There is an important group of French words that end in **-al** in the singular and which change to **-aux** in the plural.

Singular	Plural		
le journal	les journaux	*newspaper*	*newspapers*
l'animal	les animaux	*animal*	*animals*

The gender of a noun does not change when it becomes plural (see **What is Meant by Gender?**, p. 6).

Hearing the Plural

The main difference between the plural forms in English and French is that in French, even though you can see the plural ending if you are reading the word, you can rarely hear it, because the final "s" is never pronounced.

same pronunciation

livre	livres
table	tables

You will usually have to listen to the word that comes before the noun to know whether the noun is singular or plural. The examples below show you that in English you hear the plural in the noun itself, while in French you hear it in the word that precedes it.

	Singular	Plural
English	the **book**	the **books**
	the **table**	the **tables**
French	**le** livre	**les** livres
	la table	**les** tables

▼▼▼▼▼▼▼▼▼▼▼▼▼▼REVIEW ▼▼▼▼▼▼▼▼▼▼▼▼▼▼▼

Look at the English and French words below. Indicate under COLUMN A if the word is singular (S) or plural (P).
▪ Say the English and French words aloud. Indicate under COLUMN B if you can hear if the word is singular (S) or plural (P), or (?) if you can't tell.

	Column A		Column B		
1. desks	S	P	S	P	?
2. maisons	S	P	S	P	?
3. tooth	S	P	S	P	?
4. cheval	S	P	S	P	?
5. feet	S	P	S	P	?
6. étudiantes	S	P	S	P	?

4. WHAT ARE ARTICLES?

An **article** is a word placed before a noun to show whether the noun refers to a particular person, animal, place, thing, event, or idea, or whether the noun refers to an unspecified person, thing, or idea.

> I saw *the* boy you spoke about.
> a particular boy

> I saw *a* boy in the street.
> an unspecified boy

Definite Articles

IN ENGLISH

A **definite article** is used before a noun when we are speaking about a particular person, place, animal, thing, or idea. There is one definite article, *the*.

> I read *the* book you recommended.
> a particular book

> I ate *the* apple you gave me.
> a particular apple

The definite article remains *the* when the noun which follows becomes plural.

> I read *the books* you recommended.
> I ate *the apples* you gave me.

IN FRENCH

As in English, a definite article is used before a noun when referring to a particular person, place, animal, thing, or idea. However, in French, the article works hand in hand with the noun it belongs to in that it matches the noun's gender and number. This "matching" is called **agreement**. (One says that "the article agrees with the noun.") A different article is used, therefore, depending on whether the noun is masculine or feminine (gender) and depending on whether the noun is singular or plural (number). Because these articles are both pronounced and spelled differently, they indicate the gender and number of the noun to the ear as well as to the eye.

There are four forms of the definite article: three singular forms and one plural.

Le indicates that the noun is masculine singular.

le livre	*the book*
le garçon	*the boy*

La indicates that the noun is feminine singular.

la table	*the table*
la pomme	*the apple*

L' is used instead of **le** and **la** before a word beginning with a vowel. It does not tell us, therefore, if the noun is masculine or feminine.

l'étudiant   *the student*
|
masculine

l'école   *the school*
|
feminine

The letter "h" exists only in writing. It is never pronounced. When a word starts with the letter "h", the word is usually considered as beginning with a vowel: **l'herbe** *(the grass)*; **l'hôtel** (the *hotel)*. Your textbook will go into the few exceptions to this rule.

The dropping of a final vowel before a word starting with a vowel[1] is called an **elision.** You will have to rely on the dictionary or your memory to know if the word is masculine or feminine.

Les is used to indicate that the noun is plural. Since there is only one form, it does not tell us if the noun is masculine or feminine.

Masculine plural

les livres	*the books*
les garçons	*the boys*

Feminine plural

les tables	*the tables*
les pommes	*the apples*

---

[1]Vowels are the sounds associated with the letters *a, e, i, o* and *u;* consonants are the sounds associated with the other letters of the alphabet.

Indefinite Articles

IN ENGLISH

An **indefinite article** is used before a noun when we are speaking about an unspecified person, animal, place, thing, event, or idea. There are two indefinite articles, *a* and *an*.

A is used before a word beginning with a consonant.

> I saw *a* boy in the street.
> |
> not a particular boy

An is used before a word beginning with a vowel.

> I ate *an* apple.
> |
> not a particular apple

The indefinite article is used only with a singular noun; it is dropped when the noun becomes plural. At times, the word *some* is used to replace it, but it is usually omitted.

> I saw boys in the street.
> I saw *(some)* boys in the street.
>
> I ate apples.
> I ate *(some)* apples.

IN FRENCH

As in English, an indefinite article is used in French before a noun when referring to an unspecified person, animal, place, thing, event, or idea. Just as with definite articles, indefinite articles must agree with the noun's gender and number.

There are three forms of the indefinite article: two singular forms and one plural.

Un indicates that the noun is masculine singular.

> un livre   *a book*
> un garçon   *a boy*

Une indicates that the noun is feminine singular.

> une table   *a table*
> une pomme   *an apple*

Des is used to indicate that the noun is plural. Since there is only one form, it does not tell us if the noun is masculine or feminine.

Masculine plural
des livres *books*
des garçons *boys*

Feminine plural
des tables *tables*
des pommes *apples*

Partitive Articles

French also has another set of articles called **partitive articles** because they refer to *"part* of the whole." They are used before certain nouns called **non-count nouns**. As the name implies, a non-count noun designates an object that cannot be counted. It is, therefore, always singular. For example, the noun *water* is a non-count noun because it is a noun which cannot be preceded by numbers such as 1, 2, 3, etc. (You cannot count *one water, two waters...*) The opposite of non-count nouns is count nouns. A **count noun** can be singular or plural because it designates an object that can be counted. For example, the noun *pen* can be preceded by numbers such as 1, 2, 3 etc. (*one pen, two pens...*).

Like all articles in French, partitive articles agree with the noun's gender and number. Since non-count nouns don't have a plural form and are always singular, partitive articles only have singular forms.

As you will see in the examples below, French partitive articles can be translated by the words *some* or *any,* but they are often left out in English. In French, however, the partitive article must always be expressed.

There are three forms of the partitive.

Du indicates that the noun is masculine singular.

J'achète **du** beurre.
*I am buying (**some**) butter.*

Voulez-vous **du** beurre?
*Do you want (**any**) butter?*

De la indicates that the noun is feminine singular.

J'achète **de la** viande.
I am buying (some) meat.

Voulez-vous **de la** viande?
Do you want (any) meat?

De l' is used instead of **du** and **de la** before a word beginning with a vowel. It does not tell us, therefore, if the noun is masculine or feminine.

Je bois **de l'**eau.
       |
   feminine
I am drinking (some) water.

Devez-vous **de l'**argent à Marie?
             |
         masculine
Do you owe (any) money to Mary?

This form does not tell you the gender because **de l'** is used with both masculine and feminine singular nouns.

The above is a brief summary of the different forms of the partitive articles. Refer to your textbook for the rules regarding their usage.

Hearing the Gender and Number

In spoken French the gender of a noun can usually be heard only in the singular form of articles. When a noun is preceded by a definite article, the feminine gender can be heard in the "a" sound at the end of **la.** The masculine gender is harder to identify because the final "e" of **le** is not pronounced. When a noun is preceded by a definite article, you will have to train your ear to hear the difference between **un** and **une.** The number of a noun will often only be heard in the article which precedes it, **les** or **des.**

▼▼▼▼▼▼▼▼▼▼▼▼▼▼REVIEW ▼▼▼▼▼▼▼▼▼▼▼▼▼▼▼▼▼

Below is a list of English nouns preceded by a definite or indefinite article.

- Circle which of the nouns below are count nouns (C) and which are non-count nouns (N).
- Write the French article for each noun on the line provided. The French DICTIONARY ENTRY shows you if the noun (n.) is masculine (m.) or feminine (f.).

			Dictionary entry	**French article**
1. the books	C	N	livre (n.m.)	_____
2. the friend	C	N	ami (n.m.)	_____
3. some chairs	C	N	chaise (n.f.)	_____
4. an idea	C	N	idée (n.f.)	_____
5. some money	C	N	argent (n.m.)	_____
6. the weather	C	N	temps (n.m.)	_____
7. a course	C	N	cours (n.m.)	_____
8. some luck	C	N	chance (n.f.)	_____
9. the dinner	C	N	dîner (n.m.)	_____
10. some ice-cream	C	N	glace (n.f.)	_____

5. WHAT IS THE POSSESSIVE?

The term **possessive** means that one noun owns or *possesses* another noun.

The book's pages are torn.
possessor possessed
singular plural

IN ENGLISH

You can show possession in one of two ways.

1. An *apostrophe* can be used. In this construction, the noun possessor comes before the noun possessed.

   A singular common or proper noun possessor adds an apostrophe + "s".

   Mary's dress
   singular possessor

   the professor's book
   a tree's branches

   A plural possessor ending with "s" adds an apostrophe after the "s".

   the students' teacher
   plural possessor

   the girls' club

   A plural possessor not ending with "s" adds an apostrophe + "s".

   the children's playground
   plural possessor

   the men's department

2. The word *of* can be used. In this structure, the noun possessed comes before the noun possessor.

   A singular or plural common noun possessor is preceded by *of the* or *of a.*

   the book *of the* professor
   singular common noun possessor

the branches *of a* tree
the teacher *of the* students
       |
plural common noun possessor

A proper noun possessor is preceded by *of.*

the dress *of* Mary
               |
proper noun possessor

IN FRENCH

The apostrophe structure (1 above) does not exist. There is only one way to express possession and that is by using the "of" (**de**) construction (2 above).

When a noun possesses another noun the structure is as follows: the noun possessed + **de** + definite or indefinite article + the noun possessor

Mary's dress	*the dress of Mary*
| | possessor noun possessed	| | noun possessor possessed la robe **de** Marie

the professor's book	*the book of the professor*
	le livre **du** professeur
	      |
	    de + le

a tree's branches	*the branches of a tree* les branches **d'un** arbre
the lady's handbag	*the handbag of the lady* le sac **de la** dame

the students' teacher	*the teacher of the students*
	le professeur **des** étudiants
	       |
	     de + les

Careful

Do not confuse **du, de la, de l'**, and **des** meaning *of* and *of the* with words of the same spelling which are partitive articles (see p. 15) and the plural indefinite article (p. 15) meaning *some* or *any.* When they indicate possession, they usually come between two nouns *(the book of the teacher).*

▼▼▼▼▼▼▼▼▼▼▼▼▼▼▼▼REVIEW ▼▼▼▼▼▼▼▼▼▼▼▼▼▼▼▼▼

Below are possessives using the apostrophe. Write the alternate English structure which is the word-for-word equivalent of the French structure.

1. some children's parents   _____

2. the dress's color   _____

3. the school's entrance   _____

4. a car's speed   _____

5. the books' covers   _____

6. WHAT IS A VERB?

A **verb** is a word that indicates the action of the sentence. The word "action" is used in its broadest sense, not necessarily physical action.

IN ENGLISH

Let us look at different types of words which are verbs:

- a physical activity   to run, to hit, to talk, to walk, to box
- a mental activity   to hope, to believe, to imagine, to dream, to think
- a condition   to be, to sit, to have

Many verbs, however, do not fall neatly into one of the above categories. They are verbs nevertheless because they represent the "action" of the sentence.

> The book *costs* only $5.00.
> to cost

> The students *seem* tired.
> to seem

To help you learn to recognize verbs, look at the paragraph below where the verbs are in *italics.*

> The three students *entered* the restaurant, *selected* a table, *hung* up their coats and *sat* down. They *looked* at the menu and *asked* the waitress what she *recommended.* She *advised* the daily special, beef stew. It *was* not expensive. They *chose* a bottle of red wine and *ordered* a salad. The service *was* slow, but the food *tasted* very good. Good cooking, they *decided, takes* time. They *ate* pastry for dessert and *finished* the meal with coffee.

The verb is one of the most important words in a sentence; you cannot write a **complete sentence**, i.e., express a complete thought, without a verb. It is important that you learn to identify verbs because the function of many words in a sentence often depends on their relationship to the verb. For instance, the subject of a sentence is the word doing the action of the verb, and the object is the word receiving the action of the verb (see **What is a Subject?**, p. 28, and **What are Objects?**, p. 116) .

IN FRENCH
Verbs are identified the same way as they are in English.

Terms Used to Talk About Verbs

INFINITIVE – The verb form which is the name of the verb is called an infinitive: *to eat, to sleep, to drink* (see **What is an Infinitive?**, p. 23).

CONJUGATION – A verb is conjugated or changes in form to agree with its subject: *I do, he does* (see **What is a Verb Conjugation?**, p. 36).

TENSE – A verb indicates tense, that is, the time (present, past, or future) of the action: *I am, I was, I will be* (see **What is Meant by Tense?**, p. 52).

VOICE – A verb shows voice, that is, the relation between the subject and the action of the verb (see **What is Meant by Active and Passive Voice?**, p. 85).

MOOD – A verb shows mood, that is, the speakers' attitude toward what they are saying (see **What is Meant by Mood?**, p. 50).

PARTICIPLE – A verb may also be used to form a participle: *writing, written, singing, sung* (see **What is a Participle?**, p. 59).

TRANSITIVE OR INTRANSITIVE – A verb can be classified as transitive or intransitive depending on whether or not the verb can take a direct object (see **What are Objects?**, p. 116).

▼▼▼▼▼▼▼▼▼▼▼▼▼▼▼REVIEW ▼▼▼▼▼▼▼▼▼▼▼▼▼▼▼▼▼

Circle the verbs in the following sentences.

1. The students purchase their lunch at school.

2. Paul and Mary were happy.

3. They enjoyed the movie, but they preferred the book.

4. Paul ate dinner, finished his novel, and then went to bed.

5. It was sad to see the little dog struggle to get out of the lake.

6. I attended a concert to celebrate the New Year.

7. WHAT IS AN INFINITIVE?

An **infinitive** is the name of the verb.

IN ENGLISH

The infinitive is composed of two words: *to* + the dictionary form of the verb *(to speak, to dance)*. By **dictionary form,** we mean the form of the verb that is listed as the entry in the dictionary *(speak, dance)*. Although the infinitive is the most basic form of the verb, it can never be used in a sentence without another verb which is conjugated (see **What is a Verb Conjugation?**, p. 36).

> *To learn is* exciting.
>   infinitive main verb

> It's (it *is*) important *to be* on time.
>   main verb infinitive

> Paul and Mary *want to dance* together.
>   main verb infinitive

> It *has started to rain.*
> auxiliary main infinitive
> └ verbs ┘

The dictionary form of the verb, i.e., the infinitive without the *to,* is used after a verb such as *must* and *let.*

> Paul *must be* home by noon.
>   infinitive

> Her parents *let* Mary *watch* television.
>   infinitive

IN FRENCH

The infinitive form is shown by the last two or three letters of the verb called **the ending**; the English word *to* in the infinitive has no French equivalent.

danser	*to dance*
finir	*to finish*
vendre	*to sell*

These endings, called **la terminaison** in French, also tell you which group each verb belongs to:

-**er** verbs belong to the 1st group
-**ir** verbs belong to the 2nd group
-**re** verbs belong to the 3rd group

It is important for you to identify the group to which a verb belongs so you will know what pattern to follow when conjugating that verb.

Careful

When looking up the equivalent of a verb in an English-French dictionary, be sure to look for the specific meaning of the English verb. In English it is possible to change the meaning of a verb by placing short words (prepositions or adverbs) after them. For example, the verb *look* in Column A below changes meaning depending on the word that follows it:

Column A		Column B
to look for	→	to search for
		I *am looking for* a book.
to look after	→	to take care of
		I *am looking after* the children.
to look out	→	to beware of
		Look out for lions.

In French, it is impossible to change the meaning of a verb by adding a preposition or adverb as in Column A above. An entirely different verb would be used for each of the various meanings above. When consulting a dictionary, all the examples above under Column A will be found under the dictionary entry *look* (**regarder**), but you will have to search under that entry for the expression *look for* (**chercher**) or *look after* (**surveiller**) to find the correct French equivalent. Don't select the first entry under *look* and then add on the French equivalent for *after;* the result will be meaningless in French.

▼▼▼▼▼▼▼▼▼▼▼▼▼▼REVIEW ▼▼▼▼▼▼▼▼▼▼▼▼▼▼▼▼▼▼

Circle the words that you would replace with an infinitive in French.

1. Mary has nothing more to do today.

2. The students must study their lessons.

3. Paul wants to learn French.

4. They can leave on Tuesday.

5. Paul and Mary hope to travel this summer.

8. WHAT ARE AUXILIARY VERBS?

A verb is called an **auxiliary verb** or **helping verb** when it helps another verb form one of its tenses. When it is used alone, it functions as a main verb.

Mary *is* a girl.	*is*	**main verb**
Paul *has* a headache.	*has*	**main verb**
He ***has been*** *gone* two weeks.	*has*	**auxiliary verb**
	been	**auxiliary verb**
	gone	**main verb**

IN ENGLISH

There are three auxiliary verbs: *to have, to be*, and *to do*, as well as a series of auxiliary words such as *will, would, may, must, can, could* which are used to change the meaning of the main verb.

- An auxiliary is used primarily to indicate the tense of the main verb (present, past, future — see **What is Meant by Tense?**, p. 52.)

Mary *is reading* a book.	**present**
auxiliary *to be*	

Mary *has read* a book.	**past**
auxiliary *to have*	

Mary *will read* a book.	**future**
auxiliary *will*	

- The auxiliary verb *to do* is used to help formulate questions and tomake sentences negative (see **What are Declarative and Interrogative Sentences?**, p. 46 and **What are Affirmative and Negative Sentences?**, p. 43)

Does Mary *read* a book?	**interrogative sentence**
Mary *does* not *read* a book.	**negative sentence**

IN FRENCH

There are only two auxiliary verbs: **avoir** (*to have*) and **être** (*to be*). The other English auxiliary verbs such as *do, does, did, will* or *would* do not exist as separate words. In French their meaning is conveyed either by a different structure or by the form of the main verb. You will find more on this subject under the different tenses.

The verbs **avoir** and **être** are irregular verbs whose conjugations must be memorized. They are important verbs because they serve both as auxiliary verbs and main verbs.

J'ai un livre.	avoir	**main verb**
I have a book.		
J'ai pris un livre.	**avoir**	**auxiliary verb**
I have taken a book.	prendre (to take)	**main verb**
Je suis fatigué.	être	**main verb**
I am tired.		
Je suis allé à la maison.	**être**	**auxiliary verb**
I have gone home.	aller (to go)	**main verb**

The auxiliary verbs **avoir** and **être** conjugated in the different tenses and followed by the past participle of the main verb (see **What is a Participle?**, p. 59) are used to form the various tenses of the main verb. A verb tense composed of an auxiliary verb plus a main verb is called a **compound tense**, as opposed to a **simple tense** which is a tense composed of only the main verb.

Je **mange.**
simple tense
present of **manger**
I eat.

J'ai **mangé.**
auxiliary main
verb   verb
compound tense
past tense of **manger**
I have eaten.

Let us look at some examples of the compound tenses you will encounter in your study of French. (The first sentence of each pair uses a form of **avoir** as an auxiliary, and the second, a form of **être**.)

PASSÉ COMPOSÉ (PRESENT PERFECT)—Present of **avoir** or **être** + past participle of main verb (see **What is the Past Tense?**, p. 63)

Le garçon **a mangé** la pomme.
The boy ate (has eaten) the apple.

La fille **est allée** au cinéma.
The girl went (has gone) to the movies.

PLUS-QUE-PARFAIT (PAST PERFECT)—Imperfect of **avoir** or **être** + past participle of main verb (see **What is the Past Perfect Tense?**, p. 69)

> Le garçon **avait mangé** la pomme.
> *The boy **had eaten** the apple.*

> La fille **était allée** au cinéma.
> *The girl **had gone** to the movies.*

FUTUR ANTÉRIEUR (FUTURE PERFECT)—Future of **avoir** or **être** + past participle of main verb (see **What is the Future Perfect Tense?**, p. 75)

> Le garçon **aura mangé** la pomme.
> *The boy **will have eaten** the apple.*

> La fille **sera allée** au cinéma.
> *The girl **will have gone** to the movies.*

CONDITIONNEL PASSÉ (PAST CONDITIONAL)—Conditional of **avoir** or **être** + past participle of main verb (see **What is the Conditional?**, p. 77)

> Le garçon **aurait mangé** la pomme.
> *The boy **would have eaten** the apple.*

> La fille **serait allée** au cinéma.
> *The girl **would have gone** to the movies.*

You will learn other compound tenses as your study of French progresses.

▼▼▼▼▼▼▼▼▼▼▼▼▼▼REVIEW ▼▼▼▼▼▼▼▼▼▼▼▼▼▼▼▼

Cross out the English auxiliary verbs which are not used as auxiliaries in French.

1. Did the children do their homework?

2. They will do their homework tomorrow.

3. Do you want to study now?

4. Have the children done their homework?

9. WHAT IS A SUBJECT?

In a sentence the person or thing that performs the action is called the **subject**. When you wish to find the subject of a sentence, always look for the verb first; then ask, *who?* or *what?* before the verb. The answer will be the subject.[1]

Paul speaks French.
> *Who* speaks French? Answer: Paul.
> *Paul* is the subject.
> The subject is singular. It refers to one person.

Are the keys on the table?
> *What* is on the table? Answer: the keys.
> *Keys* is the subject.
> The subject is plural. It refers to more than one thing.

Train yourself to ask that question to find the subject. Never assume a word is the subject because it comes first in the sentence. Subjects can be located in several different places, as you can see in the following examples (the *subject* is in boldface and the *verb* italicized):

*Did **the game** start on time?*
After playing for two hours, **Paul** *became* exhausted.
Looking in the mirror *was* a little **girl.**

Some sentences have more than one main verb; you have to find the subject of each verb.

The **boys** *were doing* the cooking, while **Mary** *was setting* the table.

> *Boys* is the subject of *were doing*.
> (Note that the subject and verb are plural.)

> *Mary* is the subject of *was setting*.
> (Note that the subject and verb are singular.)

In both English and French it is important to find the subject of each verb to make sure that the subject and the verb agree; that is, you must choose the form of the verb that goes with the subject. (See **What is a Verb Conjugation?**, p. 36.)

---

[1]The subject performs the action in an active sentence, but is acted upon in a passive sentence (see **What is Meant by Active and Passive Voice?**, p. 85).

▼▼▼▼▼▼▼▼▼▼▼▼▼▼REVIEW ▼▼▼▼▼▼▼▼▼▼▼▼▼▼▼▼

Find the subjects in the sentences below.
- Next to Q, write the question you need to ask to find the subject of the sentences below.
- Next to A, write the answer to the question you just asked.
- Circle if the subject is singular (S) or plural (P).

1. When the bell rang, all the children ran out.

Q: _____

A: _____   S   P

Q: _____

A: _____   S   P

2. One waiter took the order and another brought the food.

Q: _____

A: _____   S   P

Q: _____

A: _____   S   P

3. The first-year students voted for the class president.

Q: _____

A: _____   S   P

4. French is a beautiful language, but it is difficult to learn.

Q: _____

A: _____   S   P

Q: _____

A: _____   S   P

10. WHAT IS A PRONOUN?

A **pronoun** is a word used in place of one or more nouns. It may stand, therefore, for a person, animal, place, thing, event, or idea.

For instance, rather than repeating the proper noun "Paul" in the following two sentences, it is better to use a pronoun in the second sentence.

> *Paul* likes to swim. *Paul* practices every day.
> *Paul* likes to swim. *He* practices every day.

Generally a pronoun can only be used to refer to someone (or something) that has already been mentioned. The word that the pronoun replaces or refers to is called the **antecedent** of the pronoun. In the example above, the pronoun *he* refers to the proper noun *Paul. Paul* is the antecedent of the pronoun *he.*

IN ENGLISH

There are different types of pronouns, each serving a different function and following different rules. Listed below are the more important types and the sections where they are discussed in detail.

PERSONAL PRONOUNS–These pronouns change their form according to the function they have in the sentence.

- as subject (see p. 32)

  > *I* go; *they* read; *he* runs; *she* sings.

- as direct object (see p. 123)

  > Paul loves *it.* Jane met *him.*

- as indirect object (see p. 126)

  > Jane gave *us* the book. Speak to *them.*

- as object of a preposition (see p. 129)

  > Paul is going out with *her.*

- as a disjunctive (see p. 133)

  > Who is there? *Me.*

REFLEXIVE PRONOUNS—These pronouns refer back to the subject of the sentence (see p. 82).

> I cut *myself.* We washed *ourselves.*

INTERROGATIVE PRONOUNS—These pronouns are used in questions (see p. 138).

> *Who* is that? *What* do you want?

DEMONSTRATIVE PRONOUNS—These pronouns are used to point out persons or things (see p. 169).

> *This* (one) is expensive. *That* (one) is cheap.

POSSESSIVE PRONOUNS—These pronouns are used to show possession (see p. 148).

> Whose book is that? *Mine. Yours* is on the table.

RELATIVE PRONOUNS—These pronouns are used to introduce relative subordinate clauses (see p. 154).

> The man *who* came is very nice.
> That is the book *which* you read last summer.

INDEFINITE PRONOUNS—These pronouns are used to refer to unidentified persons or things.

> *One* doesn't do that.
> *Something* is wrong.

The French indefinite pronouns correspond in usage to their English equivalents. They can be studied in your textbook .

IN FRENCH

Pronouns are identified in the same way as in English. The most important difference is that a pronoun agrees with the noun it replaces; that is, it must correspond in gender, and usually in number, with its antecedent.

▼▼▼▼▼▼▼▼▼▼▼▼▼▼REVIEW ▼▼▼▼▼▼▼▼▼▼▼▼▼▼▼▼

Circle the pronouns in the sentences below.
- Draw an arrow from the pronoun to its antecedent, or antecedents if there is more than one.

1. Did Mary call Peter? Yes, she called him last night.

2. The coat and dress are elegant, but they are expensive.

3. Mary baked the cookies herself.

4. Paul and I are very tired. We went out last night.

5. If the book is not on the bed, look under it.

11. WHAT IS A SUBJECT PRONOUN?

A **subject pronoun** is a pronoun used as a subject of a verb.

> *He* worked while *she* read.

> Who worked? Answer: He.
> *He* is the subject of the verb *worked.*

> Who read? Answer: She.
> *She* is the subject of the verb *read.*

Subject pronouns are divided into the following categories: the person speaking (the **first person**), the person spoken to (the **second person**), and the person spoken about (the **third person**). These categories are further divided into singular and plural.

Let us compare the personal subject pronouns in English and French.

	English	French
Singular 1st person *the person speaking*	I	**je**
2nd person *the person spoken to*	you	**tu**
3rd person *the person or object spoken about*	he she it	**il** **elle** **il** or **elle**
Plural 1st person *the person speaking plus others*	we	**nous**
Paul and I speak French. └─┬─┘ we		
2nd person *the person(s) spoken to*	you	**vous**
Paul and you speak French. └─┬─┘ you		
3rd person *the persons or objects spoken about*	they	**ils** **elles**
Paul and Mary speak French. └─┬─┘ they		

There are three English subject pronouns which have more than one equivalent in French: *you, it* and *they*. Let us look at each one so that you can learn how to choose the correct form.

"YOU" → TU OR VOUS
IN ENGLISH

You is always used to address the person or persons you are talking to. The same pronoun *you* is used to address the President of the United States or your dog.

> Do *you* have any questions, Mr. President.
> *You* are a good dog, Heidi.

Also, there is no difference between *you* in the singular and *you* in the plural. For example, if there were many people standing in a room and you asked: "Are *you* coming with me?" the *you* could refer to one person or to more than one.

IN FRENCH

There are two sets of pronouns for *you:*

1. The **familiar form**—tu singular (**vous** plural). This form is used when you speak to a child, family member, a friend, an animal, or anyone with whom you are not on formal terms.

2. The **formal form**—vous singular (**vous** plural). This form, also called the **polite form**, is used to address one or more persons you do not know very well.

When in doubt, always use the polite form, unless speaking to a child or animal, because you are likely to offend French speakers by addressing them with **tu** when it is not appropriate.

See p. 37 and p. 39 for a more detailed study of these forms.

"IT" → IL OR ELLE
IN ENGLISH

Whenever you refer to one thing or idea, you use the pronoun *it.*

> Where is the book? *It* is on the table.
> Here is the chair. *It* is comfortable.

IN FRENCH

The singular subject pronoun you use depends on the gender of the noun it replaces (see **What is Meant by Gender?**, p. 6); that is, the pronoun must correspond in gender with its antecedent.

Masculine antecedent → **il**

Où est le livre? **Il** est sur la table.
   | |
  masc. sing. masc. sing
  antecedent pronoun

Where is the book? It is on the table.

Feminine antecedent → **elle**

Voici la chaise. **Elle** est confortable.
   | |
  fem. sing. fem. sing.
  antecedent pronoun

Here is the chair. It is comfortable.

"THEY" → ILS OR ELLES

IN ENGLISH

Whenever you refer to more than one person or more than one object you use the plural pronoun *they.*

Paul and Henry are students; *they* study a lot.
Where are the books? *They* are on the table.
Here are the chairs. *They* are comfortable.

IN FRENCH

The plural subject pronoun you use depends on the gender of the noun it replaces, that is, the pronoun must correspond in gender with the antecedent.

Masculine antecedents → **ils**

Paul et Henri sont étudiants; **ils** étudient beaucoup.
 |____,____| |
 masc. pl.   masc. pl.
 antecedent   pronoun

Paul and Henry are students. They study a lot.

Où sont les livres? **Ils** sont sur la table.
   | |
  masc. pl. masc. pl.
  antecedent pronoun

Where are the books? They are on the table.

Feminine antecedents → **elles**

Voici les chaises; **elles** sont confortables.
   | |
  fem. pl. fem. pl.
  antecedent pronoun

Here are the chairs; they are comfortable.

Two or more masculine antecedents → **ils**

> Où sont le livre et le cahier? **Ils** sont sur la table.
>
> masc. sing.   masc. sing.   masc. pl.
> └ antecedents ┘   pronoun
>
> *Where are the book and the notebook?* ***They are on the table.***

Two or more feminine antecedents → **elles**

> Où sont la clé et la montre? **Elles** sont sur la table.
>
> fem. sing.   fem. sing.   fem. pl.
> └ antecedents ┘   pronoun
>
> *Where are the key and the watch?* ***They are on the table.***

Two or more antecedents of different genders → **ils**

> Voici la clé et le cahier. **Ils** sont sur la table.
>
> fem. sing.   masc. sing.   masc. pl.
> └ antecedents ┘   pronoun
>
> *Here are the key and the notebook.* ***They are on the table.***

▼▼▼▼▼▼▼▼▼▼▼▼▼▼▼REVIEW ▼▼▼▼▼▼▼▼▼▼▼▼▼▼▼▼▼

Write the French subject pronoun that you would use to replace the words in italics.
■ Write the corresponding person and number of each pronoun.

	French subject pronoun	Person	Number
1. Am I invited?	_____	_____	_____
2. Come on children, you must go to bed now.	_____	_____	_____
3. Paul and I are going out.	_____	_____	_____
4. Mommy, you have to give me a kiss.	_____	_____	_____
5. Mary and Helen are home.	_____	_____	_____
6. Do you and your wife like sports?	_____	_____	_____
7. My brother and sister speak French.	_____	_____	_____

12. WHAT IS A VERB CONJUGATION?

A **verb conjugation** is a list of the six possible forms of the verb for a particular tense. For each tense, there is one verb form for each of the six persons used as the subject of the verb. (See **What is a Subject Pronoun?**, p. 32.)

IN ENGLISH

Most verbs change very little. Let us look at the various forms of the verb to sing when each of the possible pronouns is the subject.[1]

Singular

| 1st person | I sing with the music. |
| 2nd person | You sing with the music. |

3rd person
{
He sings with the music.
She sings with the music.
It sings with the music.
}

Plural

1st person	We sing with the music.
2nd person	You sing with the music.
3rd person	They sing with the music.

Because English verbs change so little, you do not need to "conjugate verbs." It is much simpler to say that verbs add an "-s" in the 3rd person singular.

The English verb that changes the most is the verb *to be* which has three different verb forms in the present: I *am*, you/we/they *are*, he/she/it *is*.

IN FRENCH

Verb forms change constantly, and it is therefore necessary to know the form of the verb for each of the six persons for each tense. Memorizing all the forms of all the verbs that exist would be an impossible, endless task. Fortunately, most French verbs belong to the first of the following two categories:

Regular verbs whose forms follow a regular pattern. Only one example must be memorized and the pattern can then be applied to other verbs in the same group.

---

[1]In this section we will speak only about the present tense (see **What is the Present Tense?**, p. 54).

Irregular verbs whose forms do not follow any regular pattern and must be memorized individually.

Whatever verb conjugation you memorize, regular or irregular, a conjugation is always made up of a pronoun subject and the verb form that goes with that subject. The order used to list a conjugation is always the same: the singular 1st, 2nd, and 3rd persons, then the plural 1st, 2nd, and 3rd persons.

Subject

Pay special attention to the subject pronoun in this conjugation of the French verb **chanter** *(to sing).*

Singular

1st person	je chante
2nd person	tu chantes
3rd person	{ il chante
	elle chante

Plural

1st person	nous chantons
2nd person	vous chantez
3rd person	{ ils chantent
	elles chantent

Each subject represents the doer of the action of the verb.

1ST PERSON SINGULAR–The "*I* form" of the verb (the "**je** form") is used whenever the person speaking is the doer of the action.

Le matin **je chante** bien.
In the morning I sing well.

2ND PERSON SINGULAR–The "*you* familiar singular form" of the verb (the "**tu** form") is used whenever the person spoken to (with whom you are on familiar terms, see p. 33) is the doer of the action.

Jean, **tu chantes** bien.
John, you sing well.

3RD PERSON SINGULAR–The "*he, she, it* form" of the verb (the "**il, elle** form") is used when the person, thing, or idea spoken about is the doer of the action. The 3rd person singular subject can be expressed in one of three ways:

1. the third person singular masculine pronoun **il** *(he, it)* and the third person singular feminine pronoun **elle** *(she, it)*

> **Il chante** bien.
> *He sings well.*
>
> Regardez ce livre. **Il est** intéressant.
> *Look at this book. It is interesting.*
>
> **Elle chante** bien.
> *She sings well.*
>
> Voici la chaise. **Elle est** confortable.
> *Here is the chair. It is comfortable.*

2. a proper noun

> **Marie chante** bien.
> |
> elle
> *Mary sings well.*
>
> **Paul chante** bien.
> |
> il
> *Paul sings well.*
>
> In both these sentences the proper noun could be replaced by the pronoun *he* (**il**) or *she* (**elle**), so that you must use the 3rd person singular form of the verb.

3. a singular common noun

> **La fille chante** bien.
> |
> elle
> *The girl sings well.*
>
> **L'oiseau chante** bien.
> |
> il
> *The bird sings well.*
>
> In both these sentences the common noun could be replaced by the pronoun *he* (**il**) or *she* (**elle**), so that you must use the 3rd person singular form of the verb.

1ST PERSON PLURAL – The *"we* form" of the verb (the "**nous** form") is used whenever "I" (the speaker) is one of the doers of the action; that is, whenever the speaker is included in a plural or multiple subject.

Nous chantons bien.
We sing well.

Marie, Paul et moi chantons bien.
           nous

Mary, Paul and I sing well.

> In this last sentence, the subject, *Mary, Paul and I*, could be replaced by the pronoun *we*, so that in French you must use the **nous** form of the verb.

2ND PERSON PLURAL – The "*you* plural form" of the verb (the "**vous** form") is used in two instances:

1. The plural of **tu** – When two or more persons with whom you use **tu** individually are the doers of the action.

> Paul et Marie, **vous chantez** bien.
>
> > Paul, **tu chantes** bien.
> > Marie, **tu chantes** bien.
>
> *Paul and Mary, **you sing** well.*

2. The singular and plural polite form – When one or more persons whom you address formally are the doers of the action.

> Madame Dupont, **vous chantez** bien.
> *Mrs. Dupont, **you sing** well.*
>
> Monsieur et Madame Dupont, **vous chantez** bien.
> *Mr. and Mrs. Dupont, **you sing** well.*

3RD PERSON PLURAL – The "*they* form" of the verb (the "**ils, elles** form") is used when the persons, things, or ideas which are spoken about are the doers of the action. The 3rd person plural subject can be expressed in one of three ways:

1. The third person plural masculine pronoun **ils** *(they)* and the third person plural feminine pronoun **elles** *(they)*

> **Ils chantent** bien.
> *They sing well.*
>
> Regardez ces livres. **Ils sont** intéressants.
> *Look at these books. **They are** interesting.*
>
> **Elles chantent** bien.
> *They sing well.*
>
> Voici les chaises. **Elles sont** confortables.
> *Here are the chairs. **They are** comfortable.*

2. two or more proper or common nouns

> **Marie et Paul chantent** bien.
> ils
>
> *Mary and Paul sing well.*

> **La fille et le garçon chantent** bien.
> ils
>
> *The girl and the boy sing well.*

3. a plural noun.

> **Les filles chantent** bien.
> elles
> *The girls sing well.*

Verb Form

Let us look again at the conjugation of the verb **chanter** *(to sing)*, paying special attention to the verb forms. Notice that each of the six persons has a different verb form. However, when two pronouns belong to the same person there is only one verb form. For instance, the 3rd person singular has two pronouns, **il** and **elle**, but they both have the same verb form: **chante.**

je	chante
tu	chantes
il elle }	chante
nous	chant**ons**
vous	chant**ez**
ils elles }	chant**ent**

The French verb is composed of two parts:

1. The **stem** (also called the **root**), "la racine" in French, which is found by dropping the last two or three letters from the infinitive (see **What is the Infinitive?**, p. 23).

Infinitive	Stem
chanter	chant-
finir	fin-
vendre	vend-

In regular verbs the stem rarely changes throughout a conjugation.

2. The **ending,**"la terminaison" in French, which changes for each person in the conjugation of regular and irregular verbs. You will know which endings to add when you have established which group the verb belongs to.

Conjugation of Regular Verbs

Regular verbs are divided into three groups, also called **conjugations**, based on the infinitive ending.

-er	-ir	-re
1st group	2nd group	3rd group

Each of the three verb groups has its own set of verb endings for each tense (see **What is Meant by Tense?**, p. 52). You will have to memorize all the tenses of only one sample verb from each group in order to conjugate any regular verb belonging to that group. As an example, let us look more closely at regular verbs of the first group (**-er** verbs), that is, verbs like **parler** (*to speak*) and **aimer** (*to love*) that follow the pattern of **chanter** (*to sing*), conjugated above.

1. Identify the group of the verb by its infinitive ending.

> parler
> aimer   →1st conjugation or group

2. Find the verb stem by removing the infinitive ending.

> parl-
> aim-

3. Add the ending that agrees with the subject.

je parle	**j'**aime
tu parles	**tu** aimes
il parle	**il** aime
elle parle	**elle** aime
nous parlons	**nous** aimons
vous parlez	**vous** aimez
ils parlent	**ils** aiment
elles parlent	**elles** aiment

The endings for verbs belonging to the other groups will be different, but the process of conjugation will always be the same for regular verbs:

1. Identify the group of the verb by its infinitive ending.
2. Find the verb stem.
3. According to the group, add the ending that agrees with the subject.

As irregular verbs are introduced in your textbook, the entire conjugation will be given so that you can memorize them individually. Be sure to do so because many common verbs are irregular (**avoir**, *to have*, **être**, *to be*, and **faire**, *to make*, for example).

Careful
A special word must be said about the verbs of the first group. Although you can easily see the differences among the various verb forms when they are written *(parle, parles, parlent)*, they are all pronounced in the same way *(parle)*. In order to write them correctly you will have to identify the subject.

▼▼▼▼▼▼▼▼▼▼▼▼▼▼▼REVIEW ▼▼▼▼▼▼▼▼▼▼▼▼▼▼▼▼▼

Write the stem and conjugate the regular verb **porter** *(to carry, to wear)*.

Stem: _____

je _____   nous_____

tu_____   vous _____

il/elle_____   ils/elles _____

13. WHAT ARE AFFIRMATIVE AND NEGATIVE SENTENCES?

A sentence can be classified as to whether it is expressing a fact or situation that is or a fact or situation that is not.

An **affirmative sentence** expresses a fact or situation that is; it *affirms* the information.

> France is a country in Europe.
> Paul will work at the university.
> They liked to travel.

A **negative sentence** expresses a fact or situation that is not; it *negates* the information. It includes a word of negation.

> France is *not* a country in Asia.
> Paul will *not* work at the university.
> They did *not* like to travel.

IN ENGLISH

An affirmative sentence can become a negative sentence in one of two ways:

1. add the word *not* after some verbs

Affirmative	Negative
Paul is a student.	Paul is *not* a student.
Mary can do it.	Mary can*not* do it.
They will travel.	They will *not* travel.

Frequently, the word *not* is attached to the verb and the letter "o" is replaced by an apostrophe; this is called a **contraction**. The contracted form of "will not" is "won't."

> Paul *isn't* a student.
> |
>   is not

> Mary *can't* do it.
> |
>   cannot

> They *won't* travel.
> |
>   will not

2. add the auxiliary verb *do, does,* or *did + not +* the dictionary form of the main verb (*do* or *does* is used for negatives in the present

tense and *did* for negatives in the past tense—see **What is the Present Tense?**, p. 54 and **What is the Past Tense?**, p. 63)

Affirmative	Negative
We study a lot.	We *do not study* a lot.
Mary writes well.	Mary *does not write* well.
The train arrived.	The train *did not arrive*.

Frequently, *do, does,* or *did* is contracted with *not: don't, doesn't, didn't.*

IN FRENCH

The basic rule for turning an affirmative sentence into a negative sentence is to put **ne** before the conjugated verb and **pas** after that verb. (If the conjugated verb starts with a vowel, **ne** drops the e and becomes **n'**.)

Affirmative	Negative
Nous **mangeons** beaucoup.	Nous **ne** mangeons **pas** beaucoup.
	conjugated verb
We eat a lot.	*We do not eat a lot.*
Marie **écrit** bien.	Marie **n'**écrit **pas** bien.
	conjugated verb
Mary writes well.	*Mary does not write well.*
Le train est arrivé.	Le train **n'**est **pas** arrivé.
	conjugated verb
The train has arrived.	*The train has not arrived.*

The placement of **ne** and **pas** varies somewhat when an infinitive is negated and when there is an object pronoun in the sentence. Be sure to consult your textbook.

Careful

Remember that there is no equivalent for the auxiliary words *do, does, did* in French; do not try to include them in a negative sentence.

▼▼▼▼▼▼▼▼▼▼▼▼▼▼REVIEW ▼▼▼▼▼▼▼▼▼▼▼▼▼▼▼▼

Write the negative of each sentence.
- Circle the words which indicate the negative in the sentences you have just written.
- Box in the English words around which you would place the **ne . . . pas** in a French sentence.

1. We want to speak English in class.

_____

2. He does his homework.

_____

3. Helen was home this morning.

_____

4. Paul can go to the restaurant with us.

_____

14. WHAT ARE DECLARATIVE AND INTERROGATIVE SENTENCES?

A sentence can be classified according to its purpose, whether it makes a statement or asks a question.

A **declarative sentence** is a sentence that is a statement; it *declares* the information.

Columbus discovered America in 1492.

An **interrogative sentence** is a sentence that asks a question.

When did Columbus discover America?

In written language, an interrogative sentence always ends with a question mark.

IN ENGLISH
A declarative sentence can be changed to an interrogative sentence in one of two ways:

1. Add the auxiliary verb *do, does,* or *did* before the subject and change the main verb to the dictionary form of the verb (*do* and *does* are used to introduce a question in the present tense and *did* to introduce a question in the past tense—see **What is the Present Tense?**, p. 54 and **What is the Past Tense?**, p. 63).

Declarative sentence	Interrogative sentence
Philip *likes* the class.	*Does* Philip *like* the class?
present 3rd pers. sing.	present 3rd pers. sing. + dictionary form
Paul and Mary *sing* together.	*Do* Paul and Mary *sing* together?
present 3rd pers. pl.	present 3rd pers. pl. + dictionary form
Alice *went* to Paris.	*Did* Alice *go* to Paris?
past	past + dictionary form

2. Invert the normal word order of subject + verb to verb + subject. This **inversion** process can only be used with verbs that can be used as auxiliaries (see **What are Auxiliary Verbs?**, p. 25).

Declarative sentence	Interrogative sentence
Paul is home.	*Is Paul* home?
subject + verb	verb + subject
I am late.	*Am I* late?
subject + verb	verb + subject

She will come tomorrow.   *Will she come* tomorrow?

subject + *will* + main verb   *will* + subject + main verb

IN FRENCH

A declarative sentence can be changed to an interrogative sentence in one of two ways:

1. Add the expression **est-ce que** before the statement.

> Vous mangez à la maison ce soir.
> **Est-ce que** vous mangez à la maison ce soir?
> *You are eating at home this evening.*
> *Are you eating at home this evening?*

> Paul mange à la maison.
> **Est-ce que** Paul mange à la maison?
> *Paul eats at home.*
> *Does Paul eat at home?*

> Je peux manger maintenant.
> **Est-ce que** je peux manger maintenant?
> *I can eat now.*
> *Can I eat now?*

2. Use the inversion form, that is, put any subject, except **je,** after the verb. (If **je** is the subject, use the **est-ce que** form.)

When the subject is a pronoun, simply invert the verb and pronoun subject.

> Vous mangez à la maison ce soir.
> **Mangez-vous** à la maison ce soir?
> *You are eating at home this evening.*
> *Are you eating at home this evening?*

When the subject is a noun, follow these steps:

1. State the noun subject.
2. State the verb and, when writing, add a hyphen.
3. State the subject pronoun that corresponds to the gender and number of the subject (see p. 32).

> Paul est à la maison.
> **Paul** est-il à la maison?
> (word-for-word: *Paul* is *he* home?)
> *Paul is home.*
> *Is Paul home?*

La montre et la clé sont sur la table.
La montre et la clé sont-elles sur la table?
(word-for-word: *The watch and the key* are they on the table?)

> Since both subjects (**la montre** and **la clé**) are feminine, the pronoun will be feminine plural; i.e., **elles**.

The watch and the key are on the table.
Are the watch and the key on the table?

Paul et Marie chantent ensemble.
Paul et Marie chantent-ils ensemble?
(word-for-word: *Paul and Mary* do *they* sing together?)

> Since one subject is masculine *(Paul)* and the other feminine *(Marie)*, the pronoun will be masculine plural; i.e., **ils** (see p. 35).

Paul and Mary sing together.
Do Paul and Mary sing together?

Tag Questions

In both English and French when you expect a yes-or-no answer, you can also transform a statement into a question by adding a short phrase at the end of the statement. This short phrase is sometimes called a **tag**.

IN ENGLISH

The tag repeats the idea of the statement as a negative question.

> Paul and Mary sing together, *don't they?*
> The watch and the key are on the table, *aren't they?*

IN FRENCH

The words **n'est-ce pas?** can be added to a declarative sentence to turn it into a question.

> Paul et Mary chantent ensemble, **n'est-ce pas?**
> *Paul and Mary sing together, don't they?*

> La montre et la clé sont sur la table, **n'est-ce pas?**
> *The watch and the key are on the table, aren't they?*

Notice that although the English tag changes, the French expression **n'est-ce pas** doesn't change.

Careful

Make sure that you do not use the auxiliaries *do, does* and *did* when you are asking a question in French. Just like **est-ce que**, they signal a question and are not translated. Also, use only one interrogative form or the other, either **est-ce que** with no inversion of the verb and subject, or the inversion form.

▼▼▼▼▼▼▼▼▼▼▼▼▼▼▼▼REVIEW ▼▼▼▼▼▼▼▼▼▼▼▼▼▼▼▼

I. Write the interrogative form for each of the sentences below.
▪ Circle the words which indicate the interrogative in the sentences you have just written.

1. Paul and Mary studied all evening.

_____

2. His brother eats a lot.

_____

3. The girl's parents speak French.

_____

II. Let us see the different ways the declarative sentence below can be changed to an interrogative sentence in French.

My mother and father went to the movies.

1. Box in the word before which you would place **est-ce que**?

2. Circle the word after which you would place **n'est-ce pas**?

3. To use the inversion form, fill in the answers to the steps below.

4. In the space provided, fill in the answer in French.

  ▪ State the noun subject :   _____

  ▪ State the verb: _____

  ▪ State the pronoun that

   corresponds to the subject: _____ → In French: _____

15. WHAT IS MEANT BY MOOD?

Verb forms are divided into **moods** which, in turn, are subdivided into one or more tenses. The word *mood* is a variation of the word *mode,* meaning manner or way. The various grammatical moods indicate the attitude of the speaker toward what he or she is saying. For instance, if you are making a statement you use one mood, but if you are giving an order you use another. As a beginning student of French, you only have to recognize the names of the moods so that you will know what your French textbook is referring to when it uses these terms. You will learn when to use the various moods as you learn verbs and their tenses.

IN ENGLISH

Verbs can be in one of three moods:

INDICATIVE –The indicative mood is used to state the action of the verb, that is, to *indicate* facts. This is the most common mood, and most of the verb forms that you use in everyday conversation belong to the indicative mood. Most of the tenses studied in this handbook belong to the indicative mood: the present tense (see p. 54), the past tense (see p. 63), and the future tense (p. 72).

Paul *studies* French.
     present indicative

Mary *was* here.
     past indicative

They *will come* tomorrow.
      future indicative

IMPERATIVE–The imperative mood is used to give commands or orders (see **What is the Imperative?,** p. 56). This mood is not divided into tenses.

Paul, *study* French now!
Mary, *be* home on time!

SUBJUNCTIVE–The subjunctive mood is used to express an attitude or feeling toward the action of the verb. Since it stresses feelings about the fact or idea, it is "subjective" about them. (See **What is the Subjunctive?**, p. 90.) In English, this mood is not divided into tenses.

The school requires that students *study* French.
I wish that Mary *were* here.
The teacher recommends that he *do* his homework.

IN FRENCH

The French language identifies four moods.

INDICATIVE– As in English, the indicative mood is the most common, and most of the tenses you will learn belong to this mood.

IMPERATIVE–As in English, the imperative mood is used to give orders and it is not divided into tenses.

SUBJUNCTIVE–Unlike English, the subjunctive mood is used very frequently and it is divided into tenses. The French subjunctive has two main tenses: the present subjunctive and the past subjunctive. The present subjunctive is commonly used in conversation and in written French. Textbooks use the term "present subjunctive" to distinguish that tense from the "present indicative" and the "present conditional."

CONDITIONAL–French grammar also recognizes a mood called the conditional. The conditional mood (see p. 77) is frequently used to express the action of the verb as a possibility or an impossibility if a certain condition is filled. There are two tenses: the present conditional and the past conditional.

Si j'avais de l'argent, j'**achèterais** ce livre.
*If I had money, I **would buy** this book.*

Les étudiants **seraient allés** à Paris, s'ils avaient eu le temps.
*The students **would have gone** to Paris, if they had had the time.*

Textbooks use the term "present conditional" to distinguish it from the "present indicative" and "present subjunctive." If no reference is made to the mood, the tense usually belongs to the most common mood, the indicative.

16. WHAT IS MEANT BY TENSE?

The **tense** of a verb indicates the time when the action of the verb takes place (at the present time, in the past, or in the future). The word *tense* comes from the same word as the French word "temps," which means *time*.

I am eating.	**present**
I ate.	**past**
I will eat.	**future**

As you can see in the above examples, just by putting the verb in a different tense and without giving any additional information (such as "I am eating *now*," "I ate *yesterday*," "I will eat *tomorrow*"), you can indicate when the action of the verb takes place.

Tenses may be classified according to the way they are formed. A **simple tense** consists of only one verb form (I **ate**), while a **compound tense** consists of two or more verb forms (I **am eating**).

In this section we will only consider tenses of the indicative mood (see **What is Meant by Mood?**, p. 50).

IN ENGLISH
Listed below are the main tenses of the indicative mood whose equivalents you will encounter in French:

Present

I study	**present**
I am studying	**present progressive**

Past

I studied	**simple past**
I have studied	**present perfect**
I was studying	**past progressive**
I had studied	**past perfect**

Future

I will study	**future**
I will have studied	**future perfect**

As you can see, there are only two simple tenses (present and simple past), all of the other tenses are compound tenses formed by one or more auxiliaries plus the main verb (see **What are Auxiliary Verbs?**, p. 25).

IN FRENCH
Listed below are the main tenses of the indicative mood that you will encounter in French:

Present
j'étudie	*I study, I am studying*	**présent** (Present)

Past
j'étudiais	*I was studying*	**imparfait** (Imperfect)
j'ai étudié	*I have studied*	**passé composé** (Present Perfect)
j'avais étudié	*I had studied*	**passé antérieur** (Past Perfect)

Future
j'étudierai	*I will study*	**futur** (Future)
j'aurai étudié	*I will have studied*	**futur antérieur** (Future Perfect)

As you can see, there are more simple tenses than in English (Present, Imperfect, Future). The compound tenses in French are formed with the auxiliary verbs **avoir** or **être** + the past participle of the main verb.

This handbook discusses the various tenses and their usage in separate sections: **What is the Present Tense?**, p. 54; **What is the Past Tense?**, p. 63; **What is the Past Perfect Tense?**, p.69; **What is the Future Tense?**, p. 72; and **What is the Future Perfect Tense?**, p. 75.

Careful
Do not assume that tenses with the same name are used in the same way in English and in French.

17. WHAT IS THE PRESENT TENSE?

The **present tense** indicates that the action is happening at the present time. It can be:

- when the speaker is speaking   I *see* you.

- a habitual action   He *smokes* when he is nervous.

- a general truth   The sun *shines* every day.

IN ENGLISH

There are three forms of the verb which indicate the present tense, although they have slightly different meanings:

Mary *studies* in the library.   **present**
Mary *is studying* in the library.   **present progressive**
Mary *does study* in the library.   **present emphatic**

When you answer the following questions, you will automatically choose one of the above forms.

Where does Mary study?
Mary *studies* in the library.

Where is Mary now?
Mary *is studying* in the library.

Does Mary study in the library?
Yes, Mary *does study* in the library.

IN FRENCH

There is only one verb form to indicate the present tense. It is used to express the meaning of the English present, present progressive, and present emphatic tenses. In French the idea of the present tense is indicated by the ending of the verb, without any auxiliary verb such as *is* and *does*. It is very important, therefore, not to translate these English auxiliary verbs. Simply put the main verb in the present tense.

Mary **studies** in the library.
étudie

Mary **is studying** in the library.
étudie

Mary **does study** in the library.
étudie

▼▼▼▼▼▼▼▼▼▼▼▼▼▼REVIEW ▼▼▼▼▼▼▼▼▼▼▼▼▼▼▼

Fill in the proper form of the verb to read in the following answers.
▪ Write the French verb form for sentences 2 and 3.

1. What does Mary do all day?

She _____.   FRENCH VERB: **lit.**

2. Has she read *The Red and the Black?*

No, but she _____ it right now.   FRENCH VERB: _____

3. Does Mary read French?

Yes, she _____ French.   FRENCH VERB: _____

18. WHAT IS THE IMPERATIVE?

The **imperative** is the command form of a verb. It is used to give someone an order. There are affirmative commands (an order to do something) and negative commands (an order not to do something).

IN ENGLISH

There are two types of commands, depending on who is being told to do, or not to do, something.

"You" command –When an order is given to one or more persons, the dictionary form of the verb is used.

Affirmative imperative	Negative imperative
Answer the phone.	*Don't answer* the phone.
Clean your room.	*Don't clean* your room.
Talk softly.	*Don't talk* softly.

Notice that the pronoun "you" is not stated. The absence of the pronoun *you* in the sentence is a good indication that you are dealing with an imperative and not a present tense.

You answer the phone.
└──┬──┘
present

Answer the phone.
│
imperative

"We" command – When an order is given to oneself as well as to others, the phrase "let's" (a contraction of *let us*) is used followed by the dictionary form of the verb.

Affirmative imperative	Negative imperative
Let's leave.	*Let's not leave.*
Let's go to the movies.	*Let's not go* to the movies.

IN FRENCH

As in English, there are also two basic types of commands, depending on whom is being told to do, or not to do, something. However, there are three forms because the *"you"* command has both a familiar (**tu**-form) and a formal form (**vous**-form).

For the imperative, most verbs use the present tense without the subject pronoun. Your textbook will go over the few verbs that use another tense for the imperative.

"Tu" **command** – When an order is given to someone to whom one says **tu.**

Affirmative imperative	Negative imperative
Chante.	Ne chante pas.
Sing.	*Don't sing.*
Va avec Paul.	Ne va pas avec Paul.
Go with Paul.	*Don't go with Paul.*

Notice that verbs with an infinitive ending in **-er** (ex. chanter, aller, etc.) drop the final "s" of the **tu** form of the present tense (present → tu chantes, **tu** vas; imperative → chante, va).

"Vous" **command** – When an order is given to more than one person to whom one says **tu** or to one person to whom one says **vous.**

Affirmative imperative	Negative imperative
Chantez.	Ne chantez pas.
Sing.	*Don't sing.*
Allez avec Paul.	N'allez pas avec Paul.
Go with Paul.	*Don't go with Paul.*

"Nous" **command** – When an order is given to oneself as well as to others.

Affirmative imperative	Negative imperative
Chantons.	Ne chantons pas.
Let's sing.	*Let's not sing.*
Allons avec Paul.	N'allons pas avec Paul.
Let's go with Paul.	*Let's not go with Paul.*

▼▼▼▼▼▼▼▼▼▼▼▼▼▼REVIEW ▼▼▼▼▼▼▼▼▼▼▼▼▼▼▼▼

I. Change the sentences below to the imperative affirmative.

1. You should study every evening.

_____.

2. We go to the movies once a week.

_____.

II. Change the following sentences to the imperative negative.

1. You shouldn't sleep in class.

_____.

2. We don't speak in class.

_____.

III. Circle if the verb of the sentences below is in the imperative (I) or the present (P).

1. Tu lis beaucoup.	I	P
2. Parlons français.	I	P
3. Vous allez en France.	I	P
4. Ne dormons pas.	I	P

19. WHAT IS A PARTICIPLE?

A **participle** is a form of a verb which can be used in one of two ways: with an auxiliary verb to indicate certain tenses, or as an adjective or modifier to describe something.

> I *was writing* a letter.
> auxiliary participle
> └ past tense ┘

> The *broken* vase was on the floor.
> participle describing *vase*

There are two types of participles: the present participle and the past participle. As you will learn, participles are not used in the same way in English and French.

Present Participle

IN ENGLISH
The present participle is easy to recognize because it is the *-ing* form of the verb: *working, studying, dancing, playing.*

The present participle has two primary uses:

1. as the main verb in compound tenses with the auxiliary verb *to be*

> She *is singing*.
> present progressive of *to sing*

> They *were dancing*.
> past progressive of *to dance*

2. as an adjective

> This is an *amazing* discovery.
> describes the noun *discovery*

> He was a good *dancing* partner.
> describes the noun *partner*

IN FRENCH

The present participle is formed by adding **-ant** to the stem of the **nous** form of the present tense (chant**ant**, finiss**ant**, etc.)

We refer you to your textbook for the use of the present participle in French, since it is only introduced in advanced French.

Careful

Keep in mind that the French equivalents of the common English tenses formed with an auxiliary + present participle (*she is singing, they were dancing*) do not use participles in French. These English constructions correspond to a simple tense of a French verb.

She is singing. → Elle **chante.**
present progressive   present

They were dancing. → Ils **dansaient.**
past progressive   imperfect

He will be writing. → Il **écrira.**
future progressive   future

Past Participle

IN ENGLISH

The past participle is formed in several ways. You can always find it by remembering the form of the verb that follows *I have: I have spoken, I have written, I have walked.*

The past participle has two primary uses:

1. as the main verb in compound tenses with the auxiliary verb *to have*

> I *have written* all that I have to say.
> He *hasn't spoken* to me since our quarrel.

2. as an adjective

> Is the *written* word more important than the *spoken* word?
> describes the noun *word*   describes the noun *word*

IN FRENCH
Regular verbs have a regular past participle:

-**er** verbs add -**é** to the stem
-**ir** verbs add -**i** to the stem
-**re** verbs add -**u** to the stem

Infinitive	Stem	Past participle
chanter	chant-	chanté
finir	fin-	fini
répondre	répond-	répondu

You will have to memorize irregular past participles individually. As you can see in the examples below, they may be very different from the infinitive.

Infinitive	Past participle
être	été
avoir	eu
recevoir	reçu
comprendre	compris
écrire	écrit

As in English, the past participle can be used as part of a compound verb or as an adjective.

1. as the main verb in compound tenses with the auxiliary **avoir** *(to have)* or **être** *(to be)*

> Nous **avons compris** la leçon.
> *We **have understood** the lesson.*

> Paul **est allé** à la maison.
> *Paul **has gone** home.*

Many tenses are formed with the auxiliary verbs **avoir** or **être** plus the past participle of the main verb (see **What is the Past Tense?**, p. 63). These tenses are discussed under various sections of this handbook.

2. as an adjective

When the past participle is used as an adjective it must agree with the noun it modifies in gender and in number.

> *the spoken language*
> la langue **parlée**

>> *Spoken* modifies the noun *language*. Since **la langue** *(language)* is feminine singular, the word for *spoken* must be feminine singular. This is shown by adding an -**e**.

the **written** *words*
les mots **écrits**

> *Written* modifies the noun *words*. Since **les mots** *(words)* is masculine plural, the word for *written* must be masculine plural. This is shown by adding an **-s.**

▼▼▼▼▼▼▼▼▼▼▼▼▼▼REVIEW ▼▼▼▼▼▼▼▼▼▼▼▼▼▼▼▼

Circle the auxiliary + present participles in the sentences below which are the equivalent of a simple tense in French.

1. I am speaking French.

2. Paul and Mary were studying for the exam.

3. Are you bringing the book to class ?

4. The students will be trying to memorize the verbs.

20. WHAT IS THE PAST TENSE?

The **past tense** is used to express an action that occurred in the past.

IN ENGLISH
There are several verb forms that indicate the action took place in the past.

I worked	**simple past**
I was working	**past progressive**
I used to work	**with helping verb** used to
I did work	**past emphatic**
I have worked	**present perfect**[1]

The simple past is called "simple" because it is a simple tense; i.e., it consists of one word *(worked* in the example above). The other past tenses are compound tenses; i.e., they consist of more than one word, an auxiliary plus a main verb *(was working, did work,* etc.).

IN FRENCH
There are two French tenses which correspond to all the English past verbal forms listed above: **the passé composé** *(the present perfect)* and the **imparfait** *(the imperfect).*

Present Perfect (passé composé)

The **passé composé** is formed by the auxiliary verb **avoir** *(to have)* or être *(to be)* conjugated in the present tense + the past participle of the main verb (see **What are Auxiliary Verbs?**, p. 25 and **What is a Participle?**, p. 59). As in English, the past participle does not change form from one person to another.

j'ai parlé	*I spoke, I have spoken*
avoir past participle auxiliary	
nous avons parlé	*we spoke, we have spoken*
je suis allé	*I went, I have gone*
être past participle auxiliary	
il est allé	*he went, he has gone*

---

[1] A separate section is devoted to the past perfect *(I had worked)*, see p. 69.

Selection of the Auxiliary Avoir or Être

Most verbs use the auxiliary **avoir.** Therefore, it is easier for you to memorize the list of verbs conjugated with **être** and assume that all the other verbs are conjugated with **avoir.**

There are approximately sixteen basic verbs, sometimes referred to by grammar books as "verbs of motion," that are conjugated with **être.** "Verbs of motion" is not an accurate description of these verbs since some of them, such as **rester** *(to stay, to remain),* do not imply motion. You will find the "**être** verbs" easier to memorize in pairs of opposites:

aller	*to go*	≠	venir	*to come*
retourner	*to return*	≠	rester	*to remain*
entrer	*to come in*	≠	sortir	*to go out*
arriver	*to arrive*	≠	partir	*to leave*
monter	*to climb*	≠	descendre	*to go down*
		≠	tomber	*to fall*
naître	*to be born*	≠	mourir	*to die*

Verbs derived from the above verbs are also conjugated with **être: rentrer** *(to return),* **revenir** *(to come back),* and **devenir** *(to become),* among others.

Agreement of the Past Participles

The rules of agreement of the past participle depend on whether the auxiliary verb is **avoir** or **être.**

1. Agreement of past participles conjugated with **être**

When the auxiliary verb is **être,** the past participle agrees with the subject (review the section **What is a Subject?**, p. 28).

Pierre est **allé** au cinéma.
subject   past participle
└ masc. sing.┘

Peter went to the movies.

Marie est **allée** au cinéma.
subject   past participle
└ fem. sing. ┘

Mary went to the movies.

Paul et Marie sont allés au cinéma.
      | |
  subjects   past participle
      └ masc. pl. ┘
*Paul and Mary **went** to the movies.*

2. Agreement of past participles conjugated with **avoir**

When the auxiliary verb is **avoir,** the past participle agrees with the direct object if the direct object comes before the verb in the sentence (review the section on direct objects, p. 116). If the direct object comes after the verb, there is no agreement and the past participle remains in its masculine singular form. Your textbook will go over this rule in detail. In the meantime, here are a few examples showing some structures where there is agreement.

Quand avez-vous vu <u>Paul</u>? Je l'ai vu hier.
                         | |
                    dir. obj. past part.
                   └ masc. sing. ┘
*When did you see Paul? I saw **him** yesterday.*

Quand avez-vous vu <u>Marie</u>? Je l'ai vue hier.
                         | |
                    dir. obj. past part.
                   └ fem. sing. ┘
*When did you see Mary? I saw **her** yesterday.*

Quand avez-vous vu <u>Paul et Marie</u>? Je les ai vus hier.
                                 | |
                        dir. obj. past part.
                     └ masc. pl. ┘
*When did you see Paul and Mary? I saw **them** yesterday.*

Remember these two steps when using the **passé composé:**

1. Determine whether the verb takes **avoir** or **être** as the auxiliary.

2. Depending on which auxiliary verb is required, apply the appropriate rules of agreement.

Imperfect (imparfait)

The **imparfait** is a simple tense formed by adding a set of endings to the stem of the verb. The conjugation is so regular that there is no need to repeat what is in your French textbook.

There are two English verb forms that indicate that the **imparfait** should be used in French:

1. when the English verb form includes, or could include, the helping verb *used to.*

> *I **used to go** to France every year.*
> J'**allais** en France chaque année.
> |
>   imparfait

> *As a child I **went** to France every year.*
> |
>   could be replaced by *used to go*
> Comme enfant j'**allais** en France chaque année.

2. when the English verb form is in the past progressive tense, as in *was singing, were working.*

> *At 8:00 P.M. last night, I **was eating** dinner.*
> A huit heures hier soir, je **dînais**.
> |
>   imparfait

Except for these two English verb forms, the English verb will not indicate to you whether you should use the **imparfait** or the **passé composé**.

Selection of the Passé composé **or the** Imparfait

Whether to put a verb is the **passé composé** or the **imparfait** will often depend upon the context in which a sentence is used. As a general guideline, remember the following:

> **passé composé** → tells "what happened"
> **imparfait** → tells "how things used to be" or "what was going on"

Let us consider the sentence "He **went** to France." The same form of the verb, namely "went," is used in the two English answers below; however, the tense of the French verb **aller** *(to go)* will be different depending on which question the verb answers.

- "What happened?"

> QUESTION: *What **did** Paul **do** this summer?*

> ANSWER: *He **went** to France.*

> In this context, you are asking and answering the question "what happened last summer"; therefore, the verb "did do" and "went" will be in the **passé composé**.

Qu'est-ce que Paul **a fait** cet été?

passé composé

Il **est allé** en France.

passé composé

- "How things used to be"

    QUESTION: *During his childhood, where **did** Paul **go** for the summer?*

    ANSWER: *He **went** to France.*

    In this context, you are asking and answering the question "how things used to be;" therefore, the verb "did go" and "went" will be in the **imparfait**.

    Pendant son enfance, où est-ce que Paul **allait** en été?

    imparfait

    Il **allait** en France.

    imparfait

As you can see from the two French examples above, the tense of the answer will usually be the same as the tense used in the question.

- "What was going on?"

    Since the **imparfait** and the **passé composé** indicate actions that took place during the same time period in the past, you will often find the two tenses intermingled in a sentence or a story.

    *I **was reading** when he **arrived**.*

    Both actions "reading" and "arrived" took place at the same time.
    What was going on? I was reading → **imparfait**
    What happened? He arrived → **passé composé**

    Je **lisais** quand il **est arrivé**.

    imparfait   passé composé

Your French textbook will give you additional guidelines to help you choose the appropriate tense. You should practice analyzing English paragraphs. Pick out the verbs in the past and indicate for each one if you would put it in the **imparfait** or in the **passé composé**. Sometimes both tenses are possible, but usually one of the two is more logical.

▼▼▼▼▼▼▼▼▼▼▼▼▼▼▼REVIEW ▼▼▼▼▼▼▼▼▼▼▼▼▼▼▼▼▼

Circle the verbs that would be put in the **Imparfait** and underline the verbs that would be put in the **passé composé**.

Last summer, I *went* to France with my family. Everyone *was* very excited when we *arrived* at the airport. While my mother *checked* the luggage and my father *handled* the tickets, my little sister Mary *ran* away. My parents *dropped* everything and *tried* to catch her, but she *ducked* behind the counter. Finally, a manager *grabbed* her and *brought* her back to us. She *was crying* because she *was* sad she *was* *leaving* her dog for two weeks. Everyone *comforted* her and, finally, she *went* on to the plane with a smile.

21. WHAT IS THE PAST PERFECT TENSE?

The **past perfect tense** is used to express an action completed in the past before some other specific action or event occurred in the past. It is used when two actions happened at different times in the past and you want to indicate which action preceded the other. [1]

IN ENGLISH
The past participle is formed with the auxiliary *had* + the past participle of the main verb: *I had walked, he had seen,* etc.

She suddenly *remembered* that she *had forgotten* her keys.

past tense   past perfect
1   2

Both actions 1 and 2 occurred in the past, but action 2 preceded action 1. Therefore, action 2 is in the past perfect.

Don't forget that verb tenses indicate the time that an action occurs. Therefore, when verbs in the same sentence are in the same tense, the actions took place during the same period of time. In order to show that they took place at different periods of time, different tenses must be used. Look at the following examples:

The mother *was crying* because her son *was leaving.*

past tense   past perfect
1   2

Action 1 and action 2 took place at the same time.

The mother *was crying* because her son *had left.*

past progressive   past perfect
1   2

Action 2 took place before action 1.

IN FRENCH
The past perfect is called **le plus-que-parfait**. It is formed with the auxiliary verb **avoir** or **être** in the **imparfait** + the past participle of the main verb: **j'avais marché, elle était allée.** The rules of agreement of the past participle are the same as for the **passé composé** (see p. 64).

---

[1] You can compare this tense with the future perfect which is used when two actions will happen at different times in the future and you want to stress which action will precede the other (see **What is the Future Perfect Tense?**, p. 75).

A verb is put in the **plus-que-parfait** tense in order to stress that the action of that verb took place before the action of a verb in either the **passé composé** or the **imparfait**.

Observe the sequence of events expressed by the past tenses in the following time-line:

VERB TENSE:	Past Perfect	Present Perfect	Present
	Plus-que-Parfait	Passé composé	Présent
		Imparfait	
	- 2	- 1	0

TIME ACTION TAKES PLACE:
$0 \rightarrow$ now
$- 1 \rightarrow$ before 0
$- 2 \rightarrow$ before -1

Same verb tense → same moment in time

*The mother **was crying** because her son **was leaving**.*
La mère **pleurait** parce que son fils **partait**.
   imparfait   imparfait
   - 1   - 1

Two actions in the **imparfait** show that they took place at the same time in the past.

Different verb tenses → different times

*The mother **was crying** because her son **had left**.*
La mère **pleurait** parce que son fils **était parti**.
   imparfait   plus-que-parfait
   - 1   -2

The action in the **plus-que-parfait** (point - 2) occurred before the action in the **imparfait** (point - 1).

Careful

You cannot always rely on English to determine when to use the past perfect in French. In many cases, English usage permits the use of the simple past to describe an action that preceded another, if it is clear which action came first.

*The teacher **wanted** to know who **saw** the student.*
   simple past   simple past

*The teacher **asked** who **had seen** the student.*

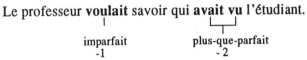

simple past   past perfect

Although the two sentences above mean the same thing and are correct in English, only the second sentence with its sequence of tenses would be correct in French.

Le professeur **voulait** savoir qui **avait vu** l'étudiant.

imparfait   plus-que-parfait
-1   - 2

Le professeur **a demandé** qui **avait vu** l'étudiant.

passé composé   plus-que-parfait
-1   - 2

The action in the **plus-que-parfait** (point -2) stresses that it was completed before the other action (point -1) which could be in the **imparfait** or the **passé composé** depending on the context of this sentence.

In French the sequence of tenses is more rigid than in English.

▼▼▼▼▼▼▼▼▼▼▼▼▼▼▼REVIEW ▼▼▼▼▼▼▼▼▼▼▼▼▼▼▼▼

In the parentheses, number the verbs according to the time-line on p. 70.
■ On the line below, indicate if the verb would be in the past (P) or past perfect (PP) in French.

1. This morning Mary read the book she bought yesterday.

(-____)   (-____)

_____   _____

2. After lunch, Paul asked who'd called him that morning.

(-____)   (-____)

_____   _____

22. WHAT IS THE FUTURE TENSE?

The **future tense** indicates that an action will take place some time in the future.

IN ENGLISH

The future tense is formed with the auxiliary *will* or *shall* + the dictionary form of the main verb. Note that *shall* is used in formal English (and British English), *will* occurs in everyday language.

> Paul and Mary *will do* their homework tomorrow.
> I *will leave* tonight.

In conversation, *shall* and *will* are often shortened to *'ll*: They*'ll do* it tomorrow; I*'ll leave* tonight.

IN FRENCH

You do not need an auxiliary to show that the action will take place in the future. Future time is indicated by a simple tense.

Regular verbs use the infinitive as the stem for the future.

Infinitive	Stem	
aimer	aimer-	*to love*
finir	finir-	*to finish*
vendre	vendr-	*to sell*
	(the final "e" is dropped)	

Irregular verbs have irregular future stems which must be memorized.

Infinitive	Stem	
aller	ir-	*to go*
venir	viendr-	*to come*
avoir	aur-	*to have*
être	ser-	*to be*

You will notice that whatever the stem, regular or irregular, the sound of the letter "r" is always heard before the future ending. Your textbook will show you how to conjugate regular and irregular verbs in the future tense.

Careful

While English uses the present tense after expressions such as *as soon as, when,* and *by the time,* which introduce an action that will take place in the future, French uses the future tense.

As soon as he returns, I will call.
present   future

Dès qu'il **reviendra**, je **téléphonerai**.
future   future

"As soon as he *will come* . . ."

She will come when she is ready.
future   present

Elle **viendra** quand elle **sera** prête.
future   future

". . . when she *will be* ready."

French is more strict than English in its use of tenses.

Immediate Future

In English and in French the fact that an action will occur some time in the future can also be expressed without using the future tense itself, but a construction which implies the future.

IN ENGLISH
You can use the verb *to go* in the present progressive + the dictionary form of the main verb: *I am going to walk, she is going to see,* etc.

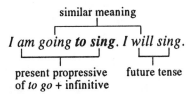

similar meaning

*I am going **to sing**. I will sing.*

present propressive   future tense
of *to go* + infinitive

IN FRENCH
The same construction exists in French. It is sometimes called **le futur immédiat** or **le futur proche** because the future action is considered nearer at hand than an action expressed by a verb in the future tense. The immediate future is formed with the verb **aller** *(to go)* in the present tense + the infinitive of the main verb: **je vais marcher, elle va voir,** etc.

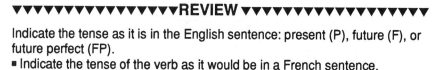

Je vais chanter.

present of **aller** + infinitive
immediate future

I am going to sing.

present of *to go* + infinitive
immediate future

Je chanterai.

future tense

I will sing.

future tense

In conversational French, the immediate future often replaces the future tense.

▼▼▼▼▼▼▼▼▼▼▼▼▼▼▼REVIEW ▼▼▼▼▼▼▼▼▼▼▼▼▼▼▼▼▼▼

Indicate the tense as it is in the English sentence: present (P), future (F), or future perfect (FP).

▪ Indicate the tense of the verb as it would be in a French sentence.

1. As soon as we finish our meal, we'll leave.

IN ENGLISH: _____ _____

IN FRENCH: _____ _____

2. We will speak French when we go to France this summer.

IN ENGLISH: _____ _____

IN FRENCH: _____ _____

23. WHAT IS THE FUTURE PERFECT TENSE?

The **future perfect tense** is used to express an action which will have happened before another action in the future or before a specific time in the future.[1]

IN ENGLISH
The future perfect is formed with the auxiliary *will have* + the past participle of the main verb: *I will have walked, she will have gone,* etc. In conversation *will* is shortened to *'ll*: or, in some cases, dropped altogether and *have* is shortened to *"'s"* or *"'ve"*.

> I'll see you as soon as I *will have finished.*
> I'll see you as soon as I'*ll have finished.*
> I'll see you as soon as I'*ve finished.*

> I'*ll call* you as soon as I'*ve found* Mary.
>   └──┬──┘   └──┬──┘
> future event   future perfect
>   2   1

> Both actions 1 and 2 will occur at some future time, but action 1 will be completed before action 2 takes place. Therefore, action 1 is in the future perfect tense.

> I *will have left* before tomorrow.
> └──┬──┘   └──┬──┘
> future perfect   future event
>   1   2

> Both action 1 and event 2 will occur at some future time, but action 1 will be completed before a specific time in the future. Therefore, action 1 is in the future perfect tense.

IN FRENCH
The future perfect is called **le futur antérieur.** It is formed with the auxiliary **avoir** or **être** in the future tense + the past participle of the main verb (the rules of agreement are the same as for the **passé composé**–see p. 64): **j'aurai marché, elle sera allée,** etc.

As in English, a verb is put in the **futur antérieur** tense in order to stress that the action of the verb will take place before the action of a verb in the future, or before a specific future time.

---

[1]You can compare this tense to the past perfect which is used when two actions occurred at different times in the past and you want to stress which action preceded the other (see **What is the Past Perfect Tense?**, p. 69).

Observe the sequence of events expressed by the future tenses in the following time-line:

VERB TENSE:	Present	Future perfect	Future
	Présent	Futur antérieur	Futur
	0	**1**	**2**

TIME ACTION TAKES PLACE: 0 → now
1 → after 0 and before 2
2 → after 0

Je vous **téléphonerai** dès que j'**aurai trouvé** Marie.

2   1

I'll call you as soon as I've found Mary.

Je **serai parti** avant demain.
I'll have left before tomorrow.

▼▼▼▼▼▼▼▼▼▼▼▼▼▼▼▼▼REVIEW ▼▼▼▼▼▼▼▼▼▼▼▼▼▼▼▼▼▼▼

In the parentheses, number the verbs according to the time line above.
▪ On the line below, indicate if in a French sentence the verb would be in the present (P), future (F), or future perfect (FP).

1. When the bell *rings* at noon, they'*ll have finished* the exam.

(   )   (   )

FRENCH TENSE: _____   _____

2. As soon as I'*ve written* the letter, I'*ll send* it.

(   )   (   )

FRENCH TENSE: _____   _____

24. WHAT IS THE CONDITIONAL?

The **conditional mood** does not exist in English, but is an important mood in French (see **What is Meant by Mood?**, p. 50). There is an English verb form however, which is similar to the French conditional and which can help you to understand it. For our purposes, we will call this form the "conditional." The conditional mood has a present and a past tense.

Present Conditional

IN ENGLISH
The "present conditional" is a compound tense. It is formed with the auxiliary *would* + the dictionary form of the main verb.

> I *would like* some ketchup, please.
> If she had the money, she *would call* him.
> I said that I *would come* tomorrow.

The "present conditional" is used in the following ways:

■ as a polite form with *like* and in polite requests

> I *would like* to eat.
> This is more polite than "I want to eat."

> *Would* you please close the door.
> The command "please close the door" is softened by the use of *would.*

■ in the main clause of a hypothetical statement

> If I had a lot of money, I *would buy* a Cadillac.

"I would buy a Cadillac" is called the **main clause,** or **result clause.** It is a clause because it is composed of a group of words containing a subject *(I)* and a verb *(would buy)* and is used as part of a sentence. It is the main clause because it expresses a complete thought and can stand by itself without being attached to the first part of the sentence ("If I had a lot of money..."). It is called the result clause because it expresses what would happen as the result of getting a lot of money.

"If I had a lot of money" is called the **subordinate clause,** or **if-clause.** It is a subordinate clause because, although it contains a subject *(I)* and a verb *(had)*, it does not express a complete thought and cannot stand alone. It must be attached to the main clause.

The entire statement is called **hypothetical** because it refers to a condition that does not exist at the present time (the person speaking does not have a lot of money), but there is the remote possibility of its becoming a reality (the person speaking could have a lot of money one day).

▪ in an indirect statement to express a future-in-the-past

An **indirect statement** repeats, or reports, but does not quote, someone's words, as opposed to a **direct statement** which is a word-for-word quotation of what someone said. In written form a direct statement is always between quotation marks.

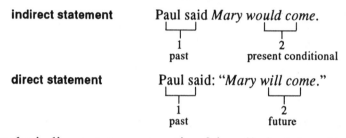

indirect statement	Paul said *Mary would come.*
	1 2
	past present conditional
direct statement	Paul said: *"Mary will come."*
	1 2
	past future

In the indirect statement, action 2 is called a **future-in-the-past** because it takes place after another action in the past. In the direct statement, action 2 is merely a quotation of what was said.

IN FRENCH
You do not need an auxiliary to indicate the present conditional, **le conditionnel présent;** it is a simple tense. It is formed with the future stem (see p. 72) + the imperfect endings: je parler**ais** (*I would speak*), il finir**ait** (*he would finish*), nous vendr**ions** (*we would sell*).

The present conditional is used in the same ways as in English:

▪ as a polite form or in polite requests

Je **voudrais** un sandwich.
present conditional
I would like a sandwich.

Pourriez-vous fermer la porte?
present conditional
Could you close the door?

- in the main clause of a hypothetical statement

> Si j'avais beaucoup d'argent, j'**achèterais** une Cadillac.
> present conditional
> *If I had a lot of money, I **would buy** a Cadillac.*

- in an indirect statement to express a future-in-the-past

> Il a dit qu'il **viendrait.**
> present conditional
> *He said (that) he **would come.***

> Je savais qu'il **pleuvrait.**
> present conditional
> *I knew (that) it **would rain.***

Careful

The auxiliary *would* does not correspond to the conditional when it stands for *used to*, as in "She *would talk* while he painted." In this sentence, it means *used to talk* and requires the imperfect (see p. 65).

Past Conditional

IN ENGLISH

The "past conditional" is formed with the auxiliary *would have* + the past participle of the main verb.

> I *would have come* if I had known.

Unlike some statements in the present conditional where there is a possibility of their becoming a reality, all statements using the past conditional are **contrary-to-fact**: the main action never happened because the condition expressed was never met and it is now over and done with.

> He *would have spoken* if he had known the truth.
> past conditional
> Contrary-to-fact: He did not speak because he didn't know the truth.

> If you had called us, we *would have come.*
> Contrary-to-fact: We did not come because you didn't call us.

> I *would have eaten* if I had been hungry.
> Contrary-to-fact: I did not eat because I wasn't hungry.

IN FRENCH

The past conditional, called **le conditionnel passé**, is formed with the auxiliary **avoir** or **être** in the present conditional + the past participle of the main verb (the same rules of agreement apply as for the **passé composé** – see p. 64): **j'aurais mangé, elle serait allée**, etc.

As in English, all statements using the past conditional are contrary-to-fact.

Il **aurait parlé**, s'il avait su la vérité.
‎   └──┬──┘
      past conditional

*He **would have spoken**, if he had known the truth.*
‎   └────┬────┘
         past conditional

Sequence of Tenses

Let us study some examples of constructions with conditions and their results so that you learn to recognize them and to use the appropriate French tense.

Hypothetical and contrary-to-fact statements are easy to recognize because they are always made up of two clauses:

- the **"If"-clause**; that is, the subordinate clause that starts with *if* (si in French)

- the **result clause**; that is, the main clause

The sequence of tenses is the same in English and in French. If you have difficulty recognizing tenses just apply these three rules.

"IF"-CLAUSE → present   RESULT CLAUSE → future
         présent   **futur**

*If he **comes**, I **will be** happy.*
‎ | └──┬──┘
  present   future

S'il **vient**, je **serai** contente.
‎ | |
  présent   futur

"IF"-CLAUSE → simple past   RESULT CLAUSE → present conditional
     imparfait   **conditionnel présent**

If he came, I would be happy.
     past   present conditional

S'il **venait,** je **serais** contente.
   imparfait   conditionnel présent

"IF"-CLAUSE → past perfect   RESULT CLAUSE → past conditional
    plus-que-parfait   **conditionnel passé**

If he had come, I would have been happy.
    past perfect   past conditional

S'il **était venu,** j'**aurais été** contente.
   plus-que-parfait conditionnel passé

In English and in French the if-clause can come either at the beginning of the sentence before the main clause, or at the end of the sentence. The tense of each clause remains the same no matter the order.

I would have been happy, if he had come.
    past conditional   past perfect

J'**aurais été** contente, s'il **était venu.**
   conditionnel passé   plus-que-parfait

▼▼▼▼▼▼▼▼▼▼▼▼▼▼REVIEW ▼▼▼▼▼▼▼▼▼▼▼▼▼▼▼▼

Write the tense you would use in French for each of the italicized verbs below: present (P), future (F) present conditional (C), past conditional (PC), imperfect (I), past perfect (PP).

1. Students *would do* their homework if they *had* time.

       ———   ———

2. If they *had had* an exam, they *would have studied.*

   ———   ———

3. When they *were* separated, he *would call* her every evening.

    ———   ———

4. We'll *be going* abroad, if we *have* the money.

     ———   ———

25. WHAT IS A REFLEXIVE VERB?

A **reflexive verb** is a verb that is linked to a special pronoun called a **reflexive pronoun;** this pronoun serves to "reflect" the action of the verb back to the performer, that is, to the subject of the sentence. The result is that the subject of the sentence and the object are the same person.

> *She* cut *herself* with the knife.
> *He* saw *himself* in the mirror.

IN ENGLISH
Many verbs can take on a reflexive meaning by adding a reflexive pronoun.

> Peter *cuts* the paper.
>   regular verb

> Peter *cuts himself* when he shaves.
>   verb + reflexive pronoun

Pronouns ending with *-self* or *-selves* are used to make verbs reflexive. Here are the reflexive pronouns.

	Subject pronoun	Reflexive pronoun
singular	I	myself
	you	yourself
	he	himself
	she	herself
	it	itself
plural	we	ourselves
	you	yourselves
	they	themselves

In a sentence a reflexive pronoun is always tied to a specific subject, because both the pronoun and the subject refer to the same person or object.

> *I* cut *myself.*
> *Paul and Mary* blamed *themselves* for the accident.

Although the subject pronoun you is the same for the singular and plural, there is a difference between the reflexive pronouns used: *yourself* is used when you are speaking to one person (singular) and *yourselves* is used when you are speaking to more than one (plural).

Paul, did you make *yourself* a sandwich?
Children, make sure you wash *yourselves* properly.

IN FRENCH
As in English many regular verbs can be turned into reflexive verbs
by adding a reflexive pronoun.

Marie **lave** son enfant.
Mary washes her child.

Marie **se lave.**
Mary washes herself.

The dictionary lists **laver** as the infinitive of *to wash* and **se laver** as
the infinitive of *to wash oneself.* Look up both forms under the verb
laver and not under **se.**

Here are the French reflexive pronouns:

me	*myself*
te	*yourself* (familiar singular)
se	*himself, herself, itself*
nous	*ourselves*
vous	*yourselves* (familiar plural, formal singular & plural)
se	*themselves*

Since the reflexive pronoun reflects the action of the verb back to the
performer, the reflexive pronoun will change as the subject of the verb
changes. You will have to memorize the conjugation of reflexive
verbs with the subject pronoun and the reflexive pronoun. For
example, let's look at the conjugation of the verb **se laver** in the present tense. Notice that unlike English where the reflexive pronoun is
placed after the verb, in French the reflexive pronoun is placed immediately before the verb.

Subject pronoun	+	Reflexive pronoun	+	Verb
je		me		lave
tu		te		laves
il elle }		se		lave
nous		nous		lavons
vous		vous		lavez
ils elles }		se		lavent

Reflexive verbs can be conjugated in all tenses. The subject pronoun and the reflexive pronoun remain the same, regardless of the tense of the verb: **ils se** *laveront* (**futur**); **ils se** *sont lavés* (**passé composé**). The perfect tenses of reflexive verbs are always conjugated with the auxiliary **être**; however, the rules of agreement for the past participle of reflexive verbs are different from the rules you apply to the past participles of non-reflexive verbs. Be sure to consult your French textbook for these rules.

Careful

Reflexive verbs are more common in French than in English; that is, there are many verbs that take a reflexive pronoun in French but not in English. For example, when you say "Paul washed in the morning," it is understood, but not stated, that "Paul washed himself." In French the "himself" must be stated: "Paul **s'est lavé.**" In addition, other English verbs such as *to get up* have a reflexive meaning: "Mary got up" means that she got herself up. In French you express *to get up* by using the verb **se lever**, that is **lever** *(to raise)* + the reflexive pronoun **se** *(oneself)*: "Marie **s'est levée.**" Memorize the many verbs that require a reflexive pronoun in French. Some of them are idiomatic expressions for which there is no direct equivalent in English.

▼▼▼▼▼▼▼▼▼▼▼▼▼▼REVIEW ▼▼▼▼▼▼▼▼▼▼▼▼▼▼

Fill in the proper English reflexive pronoun.
▪ Fill in the equivalent French reflexive pronoun in the French sentences.

1. The children wash_____every evening.

   Les enfants _____ lavent tous les soirs.

2. Mary cuts _____ constantly.

   Marie _____ coupe constamment.

3. Mary, you cut _____ constantly.

   Marie, tu _____ coupes constamment.

4. We dress _____.

   Nous _____ habillons.

26. WHAT IS MEANT BY ACTIVE AND PASSIVE VOICE?

The voice of the verb refers to a basic relationship between the verb and its subject. There are two voices: active and passive.

Active voice – A sentence is said to be in the active voice when the subject is the performer of the verb. In this instance, the verb is called an **active verb**.

> The teacher prepares the exam.
>   S   V   DO

> Paul ate an apple.
> S   V   DO

> Lightning has struck the tree.
> S   V   DO

In all these examples the subject (S) performs the action of the verb (v) and the direct object (DO) is the receiver of the action (see **What are Objects?**, p. 116).

Passive voice—A sentence is said to be in the passive voice when the subject is the receiver of the action. In this instance, the verb is called a **passive verb**.

> The exam is prepared by the teacher.
> S   V   Agent

> The apple was eaten by Paul.
> S   V   Agent

> The tree has been struck by lightning.
> S   V   Agent

In all these examples, the subject is the receiver of the action of the verb. The performer of the action, if it is mentioned, is introduced by the word "by" and is called the **agent.**

IN ENGLISH

The passive voice is expressed by the verb *to be* conjugated in the appropriate tense + the past participle of the main verb. The tense of the passive sentence is indicated by the tense of the verb *to be*.

> The exam *is prepared* by the teacher.
>   present

> The exam *was prepared* by the teacher.
>   past

The exam *will be* prepared by the teacher.

future

IN FRENCH

As in English, a passive verb is expressed by the auxiliary être *(to be)* conjugated in the appropriate tense + the past participle of the main verb. The tense of the passive sentence is indicated by the tense of the verb être.[1]

L'examen est préparé par le professeur.

present

The exam is prepared by the teacher.

L'examen a été préparé par le professeur.

passé composé

The exam has been prepared by the teacher.

L'examen sera préparé par le professeur.

future

The exam will be prepared by the teacher.

Because the auxiliary in the passive voice is always "**être**" *(to be)*, all past participles in a passive sentence agree in gender and number with the subject.

Les vins français sont **appréciés** dans le monde entier

subject → masc. pl.   past participle → masc. pl.

French wines are appreciated the world over.

Changing an Active Sentence to a Passive Sentence

The steps to change an active sentence to a passive sentence are the same in English and in French.

1. The direct object of the active sentence becomes the subject of the passive sentence.

---

[1] Verbs that take être as an auxiliary to form compound tenses in the active voice (see p. 64) do not have a passive voice since they are never followed by a direct object in the active voice. For example, **aller, partir, venir,** etc. cannot be made passive.

active   The teacher prepares *the exam.*
                                       |
                                direct object

passive   *The exam* is prepared by the teacher.
                     |
                  subject

2. The tense of the verb of the active sentence is reflected in the tense
   of the verb to be in the passive sentence.

active   The teacher *prepares* the exam.
                                   |
                                present

passive   The exam *is* prepared by the teacher.
                          |
                       present

active   The teacher *prepared* the exam.
                                   |
                                 past

passive   The exam *was* prepared by the teacher.
                          |
                        past

active   The teacher *will* prepare the exam.
                              |
                            future

passive   The exam *will be* prepared by the teacher.
                         └──┬──┘
                          future

3. The subject of the active sentence becomes the agent of the passive
   sentence introduced with *by.* The agent is often omitted.

active   *The teacher* prepares the exam.
                      |
                   subject

passive   The exam is prepared *by the teacher.*
                                     └──────┬──────┘
                                          agent

Avoiding the Passive Voice in French

Although French has a passive voice, it does not favor its use as English does, and whenever possible French speakers try to avoid the passive construction by replacing it with an active one. This is particularly true for general statements, that is, when we don't know who is doing the action.

English *is spoken* in many countries.
We don't know who is speaking.

The New York Times *is sold* here.
We don't know who is selling.

There are two ways a passive sentence can be avoided in French.

1. by using the **on** construction

The word **"on"** corresponds to the English indefinite pronoun *"one,"* as in the sentence, *"One* should eat when *one* is hungry." To avoid a passive construction, French often makes *one* the subject of an active sentence, even in sentences where English speakers would never use such a construction.

> English *is spoken in many countries.*
> **On parle** anglais dans beaucoup de pays.
> (word-for-word: *"one speaks* English in many countries")

> *The New York Times* **is sold** here.
> **On vend** le New York Times ici.
> (word-for-word: *"one sells* the New York Times here")

2. by using the reflexive verb construction

The main verb of the sentence is changed from the passive voice to its reflexive form (see **What is a Reflexive Verb?**, p. 82). This reflexive construction exists only in French and is usually senseless in English.

> English *is spoken in many countries.*
> L'anglais **se parle** dans beaucoup de pays.
> "speaks itself"

> *The New York Times* **is sold** here.
> Le New York Times **se vend** ici.
> "sells itself"

Careful

Make sure you distinguish between the auxiliary **être** + a past participle used to form a present tense in the passive voice and the auxiliary **être** + a past participle to form a past tense in the active voice. For instance, **"est mangé"** *(is eaten)* is a present tense in the passive voice, but **"est allé"** *(went)* is a past tense in the active voice.

▼▼▼▼▼▼▼▼▼▼▼▼▼▼REVIEW ▼▼▼▼▼▼▼▼▼▼▼▼▼▼▼▼

Underline the subjects in the sentences below.
- Circle the performer of the action.
- Identify each sentence as active (Ac) or passive (Pa).
- Identify the tense of the verb: past (PP), present (P), future (F).

1. The cow jumped over the moon.　　Ac　　Pa　　PP　　P　　F

2. The bill was paid by Bob's parents.　Ac　　Pa　　PP　　P　　F

3. The bank is transferring the money.　Ac　　Pa　　PP　　P　　F

4. Everyone will be going away during the vacation.

　　　　　　　　　　　　　　Ac　　Pa　　PP　　P　　F

5. The spring break will be enjoyed by all.

　　　　　　　　　　　　　　Ac　　Pa　　PP　　P　　F

27. WHAT IS THE SUBJUNCTIVE?

The **subjunctive** is a mood used to express a wish, hope, uncertainty or other similar attitude toward a fact or an idea. Since it stresses the speaker's feelings about the fact or idea, it is usually *subjective* about them.

IN ENGLISH

The subjunctive is only used in very few constructions. The subjunctive verb form is difficult to recognize because it is spelled like other tenses of the verb.

> I *am* in Paris right now.
> indicative present *to be*

> I wish I *were* in Paris right now.
> subjunctive spelled like a past tense form of *to be*

> He *reads* a book a week.
> indicative present *to read*

> The course requires that he *read* a book a week.
> subjunctive spelled like the dictionary form of *to read*

IN FRENCH

The subjunctive is used very frequently, but unfortunately English usage will rarely help you decide where and how to use it in French. Therefore, we refer you to your French textbook. First, learn how to conjugate regular and irregular verbs in the present tense of the subjunctive. (The other tenses of the subjunctive are rarely used, particularly in conversation.) Then, learn the verbs and expressions that require you to put the verb which follows in the subjunctive.

1. Example of a verb of desire that is followed by a verb in the subjunctive: **vouloir** *(to want)*

> Je veux que tu sois sage.
> **vouloir**   subjunctive être
>
> *I want you to be good.*
> (word-for-word: "I want that you *be* good")

2. Example of an expression that is followed by a verb in the subjunctive: **il faut que** *(it is necessary that)*

> Il faut que Paul **sache** parler français.
> subjunctive **savoir**
> *Paul must **know how** to speak French.*
> (word-for-word: "it is necessary that Paul *know how* to speak French")

3. Example of an adjective expressing an emotion which is followed by a verb in the subjunctive: **être heureux** *(to be happy)*

> Je suis heureux que vous **veniez** ce soir.
> subjunctive **venir**
> *I am happy that you **are coming** this evening.*

28.WHAT IS AN ADJECTIVE?

An **adjective** is a word that describes a noun or a pronoun.

IN ENGLISH

Adjectives are classified according to the way they describe a noun or pronoun.

DESCRIPTIVE ADJECTIVE – A descriptive adjective indicates a quality, it tells what kind it is. See p. 93.

> She read an *interesting* book.
> He has *brown* eyes.

POSSESSIVE ADJECTIVE – A possessive adjective shows possession, it tells whose it is. See p. 96.

> *His* book is lost.
> *Our* parents are away.

INTERROGATIVE ADJECTIVE – An interrogative adjective asks a question about someone or something. See p. 101.

> *What* book is lost?
> *Which* parents did you speak to?

DEMONSTRATIVE ADJECTIVE – A demonstrative adjective points out someone or something. See p. 103.

> *This* teacher is excellent.
> *That* question is very appropriate.

In all these cases the adjective describes, or modifies, the noun or pronoun.

IN FRENCH

Adjectives are classified in the same way as in English. The principal difference between English and French adjectives is that in English adjectives do not change their form, while in French adjectives agree in gender and number with the noun or pronoun they modify.

29. WHAT IS A DESCRIPTIVE ADJECTIVE?

A **descriptive adjective** is a word that indicates a quality of a noun or pronoun. As the name implies, it *describes* the noun or pronoun.

IN ENGLISH

The descriptive adjective does not change form, regardless of the noun or pronoun it modifies.

> The students are *intelligent*.
> She is an *intelligent* person.

The adjective *intelligent* is the same although the persons described are different in number *(students* is plural and *person* is singular).

Descriptive adjectives are divided into two groups depending on how they are connected to the noun they modify.

1. **Predicate adjective** – A predicate adjective is connected to the noun it describes (the subject of the sentence) by a linking verb, usually a form of *to be.*

> The children are *good*.
> | | |
>   noun   linking predicate
>   subject verb   adjective

> The house looks *small*.
> | | |
>   noun   linking predicate
>   subject verb   adjective

2. **Attributive adjective** – An attributive adjective is connected directly to the noun it describes and always precedes it.

> The *good* children were praised.
> | |
> attributive noun
> adjective described

> The family lives in a *small* house.
> | |
>   attributive noun
>   adjective described

IN FRENCH

The most important difference between descriptive adjectives in French and English is that in French they change forms. In French, an adjective, predicate or attributive, always agrees with the noun or pronoun it modifies; that is, it must correspond in gender and number to its noun. Thus, before writing an adjective you will have to determine if the noun or pronoun it modifies is masculine or feminine, singular or plural.

Most adjectives add an **"-e"** to the masculine form to make the feminine form and an **"-s"** to the feminine or masculine to make it plural.

the blue book	le livre **bleu**
	masc.　masc.
	sing.　sing.
the blue dress	la robe **bleue**
	fem.　fem.
	sing.　sing.
the blue books	les livres **bleus**
	masc.　masc.
	pl.　pl.
the blue dresses	les robes **bleues**
	fem.　fem.
	pl.　pl.

As you can see in the examples above, in English, the adjective "blue" comes before the noun it modifies, whereas **"bleu"** goes after the noun in French. This is not always the case, some French adjectives also come before the noun they modify. Refer to your textbook to learn whether a French adjective is placed before or after the noun it modifies.

Nouns Used as Adjectives

IN ENGLISH
You should also be able to recognize nouns used as adjectives; that is, a noun used to modify another noun. When a noun is used to describe another noun, the structure is as follows: the describing noun (adjective) + the noun described.

French is difficult.	The *French* class is interesting.
noun	adjective　noun described
Chemistry is difficult.	The *chemistry* books are expensive.
noun	adjective　noun described

IN FRENCH
When a noun is used as an adjective, that is, to describe another noun, the structure is as follows: the noun described + **de** + the describing noun (adjective) without an article. The describing noun remains a noun and does not change its form.

the French class
le français   la classe
sing.   sing.

la classe de français
fem.   masc.

the chemistry books
la chimie   les livres

les livres de chimie
masc. pl.   fem. sing.

▼▼▼▼▼▼▼▼▼▼▼▼▼▼▼REVIEW ▼▼▼▼▼▼▼▼▼▼▼▼▼▼▼▼

Circle the adjectives in the sentences below.
▪ Draw an arrow from the adjective you circled to the noun or pronoun described.

1. The young man was reading a French newspaper.

2. She looked pretty in her long red dress.

3. It is interesting.

4. The old piano could still produce good music.

5. Paul was tired after his long walk.

30. WHAT IS A POSSESSIVE ADJECTIVE?

A **possessive adjective** is a word which describes a noun by showing who possesses the thing or person being discussed. The owner is called the "possessor" and the noun modified is called the person or thing "possessed."

Whose house is that? It's *my* house.

My is an adjective that tells us who is the possessor of the noun "house."

IN ENGLISH

Here is a list of the possessive adjectives:

Singular possessor

1st person		my
2nd person		your
3rd person	{ masculine	his
	feminine	her
	neuter	its

Plural possessor

1st person	our
2nd person	your
3rd person	their

Possessive adjectives never change their form, regardless of the thing possessed; they only refer to the possessor.

Is that your house? Yes, it is *my* house.
Are those your keys? Yes, they are *my* keys.

The same possessive adjective *(my)* is used, although the objects possessed are different in number *(house* is singular, *keys* is plural).

What color is John's car? *His* car is blue.
What color is Mary's car? *Her* car is blue.

Although the object possessed is the same *(car)*, the possessive adjective is different because the possessor is different *(John* masculine singular, *Mary* feminine singular).

IN FRENCH
Like English, a French possessive adjective refers to the possessor, but unlike English, it must agree, like all French adjectives, in gender and number with the noun it modifies, that is, the person or object possessed.

For example, in the phrase **mon frère** *(my brother)* the first letter of the possessive adjective **m-** refers to the 1st person singular possessor *my*, while the ending **-on** is masculine singular to agree with **frère**, which is masculine singular. Let us see what happens when we make *my brother* plural.

> *I love my brothers.*
> J'aime mes frères.
>   masc.pl. endings
> 1st pers. sing. possessor

Let us look at the French possessive adjectives to see how they are formed. Because the rules for the selection of possessive adjectives for a singular possessor are different from the rules for the selection of possessive adjectives for plural possessors, we have the divided the French possessive adjectives into these two groups.

Singular Possessor: my, your (tu form), his, her, its

In French, each of these possessive adjectives has three forms depending on the gender and number of the noun possessed:

1. the masculine singular
2. the feminine singular
3. the plural (the same for both genders)

Here are the steps you should follow in choosing the correct possessive adjective.

1. Indicate the possessor with the first letter of the possessive adjective.

my	**m-**
your	**t-**
(**tu** form)	
his	
her }	**s-**
its	

2. Choose the ending according to the gender and number of the noun possessed.

- noun possessed is masculine singular or feminine singular beginning with a vowel → add **-on**

Hélène lit **mon** livre.	*Helen reads **my** book.*
masc. sing.	noun possessed singular
Hélène lit **ton** livre.	*Helen reads **your** book.*
Hélène lit **son** livre.	*Helen reads **her** (**his**) book.*

Paul rencontre **mon** amie.	*Paul meets **my** friend.*
fem. sing. begins with vowel	noun possessed singular
Paul rencontre **ton** amie.	*Paul meets **your** friend.*
Paul rencontre **son** amie.	*Paul meets **his** (**her**) friend.*

- noun possessed is feminine singular beginning with a consonant → add **-a**

Paul lit **ma** lettre.	*Paul reads **my** letter.*
fem. sing.	noun possessed singular
Paul lit **ta** lettre.	*Paul reads **your** letter.*
Paul lit **sa** lettre.	*Paul reads **his** (**her**) letter.*

- noun possessed is plural → add **-es**

Hélène lit **mes** livres.	*Helen reads **my** books.*
masc. pl.	noun possessed plural
Paul lit **tes** lettres.	*Paul reads **your** letters.*
fem. pl.	
Elle lit **ses** livres.	*She is reading **her** (**his**) books.*
masc. pl.	

3. Select the proper form according to the two steps above.

Let us apply the above steps to some examples:

> *Paul is looking at **his** mother.*
>   1. Possessor : s-
>   2. Noun possessed: **La mère** *(mother)* is feminine singular.
>   3. Selection: **sa**
> Paul regarde **sa** mère.

*Paul is looking at **his** father.*
1. Possessor : **s-**
2. Noun possessed: **Le père** *(father)* is masculine singular.
3. Selection: **son**
Paul regarde **son** père.

Plural Possessor: our, your (vous form), their

In French, each of these possessive adjectives has only two forms depending on the number of the noun possessed: 1. the singular (the same for both genders), and 2. the plural (the same for both genders).

■ noun possessed is singular → **notre, votre,** or **leur**

Marie est **notre** fille.	*Mary is **our** daughter.*

noun possessed singular

Paul lit **votre** lettre.	*Paul reads **your** letter.*
Ils lisent **leur** lettre	*They read **their** letter.*

■ noun possessed is plural → **nos, vos,** or **leurs**

Pierre et Marie sont **nos** enfants.	*Peter and Mary are **our** children.*

noun possessed plural

Hélène lit **vos** livres.	*Helen reads **your** books.*
Elles lisent **leurs** lettres.	*They read **their** letters.*

Careful

In French and in English, the subject and the possessive adjective do not necessarily match. It all depends on what you want to say.

Avez-**vous** **mon** livre?	*Do **you** have **my** book?*
2nd 1st	2nd 1st
pers. pers.	pers. pers.

Also, before you write a sentence with the possessive adjective *your,* decide whether it is appropriate to use the **tu** form or the **vous** form in French. Then make sure that every word that refers to "you" is in the right form, including the verb. *"You* are reading *your* letter" would be either "**Tu lis ta** lettre" or "**Vous lisez votre** lettre."

Summary

Here is a chart you can use as a reference.

Possessor		Noun possessed	
Singular		**Singular**	**Plural**
my	masc.	mon	mes
	fem. + vowel	mon	mes
	fem.	ma	mes
your	masc.	ton	tes
(tu form)	fem. + vowel	ton	tes
	fem.	ta	tes
his, her, its	masc.	son	ses
	fem.+ vowel	son	ses
	fem.	sa	ses
Plural			
our		notre	nos
your		votre	vos
(vous form)			
their		leur	leurs

▼▼▼▼▼▼▼▼▼▼▼▼▼▼▼REVIEW ▼▼▼▼▼▼▼▼▼▼▼▼▼▼▼▼

Circle the possessive adjectives in the sentences below.
- Draw an arrow from the possessive adjective to the noun it modifies.
- Circle the number of the possessive adjective: singular (S) or plural (P).
- Using the charts in this section, fill in the French possessive adjective in the French sentences below.

1. I took my books home.

POSSESSIVE ADJECTIVE IN FRENCH: masculine   S   P

J'ai pris _____ livres à la maison.

2. Mary borrowed your (familiar) car.

POSSESSIVE ADJECTIVE IN FRENCH: feminine   S   P

Marie a emprunté _____ voiture.

3. Paul looks like our mother.

POSSESSIVE ADJECTIVE IN FRENCH: feminine   S   P

Paul ressemble à _____ mère.

4. Your clothes are expensive.

POSSESSIVE ADJECTIVE IN FRENCH: masculine   S   P

_____ vêtements sont chers.

31. WHAT IS AN INTERROGATIVE ADJECTIVE?

An **interrogative adjective** is a word that asks for more information about a noun.

IN ENGLISH
The words *which* and *what* are called interrogative adjectives when they come in front of a noun and are used to ask a question about that noun.

>*Which* teacher is teaching the course?
>*What* courses are you taking?

IN FRENCH
There is only one interrogative adjective **quel** which changes to agree in gender and number with the noun it modifies. Therefore, in order to say *"which* book" or *"what* dress" in French, you start by determining the gender and number of the word *book* or *dress*.

Noun modified is masculine singular → **quel**

>**Quel** livre est sur la table?
>Livre *(book)* is masculine singular,
>so the word for "what" must be masculine singular.
>*What book is on the table?*

Noun modified is masculine plural → **quels**

>**Quels** livres sont sur la table?
>Livres *(books)* is masculine plural,
>so the word for "what" must be masculine plural.
>*What books are on the table?*

Noun modified is feminine singular → **quelle**

>**Quelle** robe portez-vous?
>Robe *(dress)* is feminine singular,
>so the word for "which" must be feminine singular.
>*Which dress are you wearing?*

Noun modified is feminine plural → **quelles**

>**Quelles** robes voulez-vous?
>Robes *(dresses)* is feminine plural,
>so the word for "which" must be feminine plural.
>*Which dresses do you want?*

In the sentences above, the interrogative adjective immediately precedes the noun it modifies. This is not always the case. As you will see below, the interrogative adjective can be separate from the noun it modifies. You must learn to find that noun, because the interrogative adjective agrees with it no matter where it is placed in the sentence.

> **What** *is your address?*
> To establish which word the interrogative adjective modifies,
> the sentence can be restructured to read: "What address is yours?"
> **Quelle** est votre adresse?
> └────┬────┘
>   fem. sing.

> **What** *are his favorite programs?*
> To establish which word the interrogative adjective modifies,
> the sentence can be restructured to read: "What programs are his favorites?"
> **Quels** sont ses programmes préférés?
> └────┬────┘
>   masc. pl.

Careful

The word *what* is not always an interrogative adjective. In the sentence *"What is on the table?"* it is an interrogative pronoun. It is important that you distinguish one from the other, because in French different words are used and they follow different rules. (See **What is an Interrogative Pronoun?**, p. 138.)

▼▼▼▼▼▼▼▼▼▼▼▼▼REVIEW ▼▼▼▼▼▼▼▼▼▼▼▼▼▼▼▼

Circle the interrogative adjectives in the sentences below.
- Draw an arrow from the interrogative adjective to the noun it modifies.
- Indicate if the noun modified is singular (S) or plural (P).
- Fill in the French interrogative adjective in the French sentences below.

1. Which courses are you taking?

   NOUN MODIFIED IN FRENCH: masculine   S   P

   _____ cours suivez-vous?

2. What is your favorite city?

   NOUN MODIFIED IN FRENCH: feminine   S   P

   _____ est ta ville préférée?

32. WHAT IS A DEMONSTRATIVE ADJECTIVE?

A **demonstrative adjective** is a word used to point out a person or an object.

IN ENGLISH
The demonstrative adjectives are *this* and *that* in the singular and *these* and *those* in the plural. They are rare examples of adjectives agreeing in number with the noun they modify: *this* changes to *these* and *that* changes to *those* when they modify a plural noun.

Singular	Plural
this cat	*these* cats
that man	*those* men

This and *these* refer to a person or object near the speaker, and *that* and *those* refer to a person or object away from the speaker.

IN FRENCH
There is only one demonstrative adjective **ce** which changes to agree in gender and number with the noun it modifies. Therefore, in order to say *"that* book" or *"this* dress" in French, you start by determining the gender and number of the word *book* or *dress*.

Noun modified is masculine singular and starts with a consonant → **ce**

> Ce livre est sur la table.
> **Livre** *(book)* is masculine singular,
> so the word for "this" must be masculine singular.
> *This (or that) book is on the table.*

Noun modified is masculine singular and starts with a vowel → **cet**

> Cet appartement est grand.
> **Appartement** *(apartment)* is masculine singular.
> Since it begins with a vowel, the word for "this" must be **cet.**
> *This (or that) apartment is large.*

Noun modified is feminine singular → **cette**

> Cette robe est jolie.
> **Robe** *(dress)* is feminine singular,
> so the word for "this" must be feminine singular.
> *This (or that) dress is pretty.*

Cette Américaine étudie le français.
 Américaine *(American girl)* is feminine singular,
 so the word for "this" must be feminine singular.
This (or that) American girl is studying French.

Noun modified is plural → **ces**

Ces livres sont sur la table.
 Livres *(books)* is plural,
 so the word for "those" must be plural.
These (or those) books are on the table.

To distinguish between what is close to the speaker *(this, these)* from what is far from the speaker *(that, those)*, **-ci** and **-là** can be added after the noun: **-ci** indicates that the noun is close to the speaker; **-là** that the noun is far from the speaker.

Ces livres-**ci** sont chers; **ces** livres-**là** ne sont pas chers.
These books (here) are expensive; those books (there) are not expensive.

▼▼▼▼▼▼▼▼▼▼▼▼▼▼▼REVIEW ▼▼▼▼▼▼▼▼▼▼▼▼▼▼▼▼
Circle the demonstrative adjectives in the sentences below.
▪ Draw an arrow from the demonstrative adjective to the noun it modifies.
▪ Circle if the noun modified is singular (S) or plural (P).
▪ Fill in the French demonstrative adjective in the French sentences below.

1. They prefer that restaurant.

 NOUN MODIFIED IN FRENCH: masculine   S   P

Ils préfèrent _____ restaurant.

2. This test is too hard.

 NOUN MODIFIED IN FRENCH: masculine   S   P

_____ examen est trop difficile.

3. These houses are expensive.

 NOUN MODIFIED IN FRENCH: feminine   S   P

_____ maisons sont chères.

33. WHAT IS MEANT BY COMPARISON OF ADJECTIVES?

We compare adjectives when two or more nouns have the same quality (height, size, color, any characteristic), and we want to indicate that one of these nouns has a greater, lesser, or equal degree of this quality.[1]

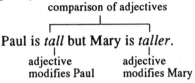

comparison of adjectives

Paul is *tall* but Mary is *taller*.

adjective   adjective
modifies Paul   modifies Mary

Both in English and in French there are two types of comparison: comparative and superlative.

Comparative

The comparative compares a quality of one person or thing with the same quality in another person or thing. The comparison can indicate that one or the other has more, less, or the same amount of the quality.

IN ENGLISH

Let's go over the three degrees of comparison:

Greater degree – The comparison of greater degree (more) is formed differently depending on the length of the adjective being compared:

- short adjective + *-er* + *than*

    Paul is tall*er than* Mary.
    Mary is pretti*er than* her sister.

- *more* + longer adjective + *than*

    Paul is *more* intelligent *than* Mary.
    My car is *more* expensive *than* your car.

Lesser degree – The comparison of lesser degree (less) is formed as follows: *not as* + adjective *as*, or *less* + adjective + *than*

    Paul is *not as* tall *as* Mary.
    My car is *less* expensive *than* your car.

Equal degree – The comparison of equal degree (same) is formed as follows: *as* + adjective + *as*

    Paul is *as* tall *as* Mary.
    My car is *as* expensive *as* your car.

---

[1]In English and in French, the structure for comparing adverbs (see **What is an Adverb?**, p. 109) is the same as the structure for comparing adjectives.

IN FRENCH

There are the same three degrees of comparison of adjectives as in English. Remember that, in French, agreement between the adjective and the noun is always required. However, since a comparative adjective always describes more than one noun, it always agrees in gender and number with the subject.

Greater degree – The comparison of greater degree is formed as follows: **plus** *(more)* + adjective + **que**

> Paul est **plus** actif **que** Marie.
> |
> agrees with Paul
> *Paul is **more** active **than** Mary.*

Lesser degree – The comparison of lesser degree is formed as follows: **moins** *(less)* + adjective + **que**

> Marie est **moins** active **que** Paul.
> |
> agrees with Marie
> *Mary is **less** active **than** Paul.*

Equal degree – The comparison of equal degree is formed as follows: **aussi** *(as)* + adjective + **que**

> Marie est **aussi** active **que** Paul.
> *Mary is **as** active **as** Paul.*

Superlative

The superlative is used to stress the highest and lowest degrees of a quality.

IN ENGLISH

Let's go over the two degrees of the superlative.

Greatest degree – The superlative of highest degree is formed differently depending on the length of the adjective:

- *the* + short adjective + *-est*

> Mary is *the* smart*est*.
> My car is *the* cheap*est* on the market.

- *the most* + long adjective

> Mary is *the most* intelligent.
> His car is *the most* expensive of all.

Lowest degree – The superlative of lowest degree is formed as follows: *the least* + adjective

Paul is *the least* active.
His car is *the least* expensive of all.

IN FRENCH
There are the same two degrees of the superlative.

Greatest degree – The superlative of highest degree is formed as follows: **le, la,** or **les** (depending on the gender and number of the noun described) + **plus** *(most)* + adjective.

Marie est **la plus** active de la famille.
fem. sing.
Mary is the most active in the family.

Paul est **le plus** grand.
masc. sing.
Paul is the tallest.

Marie et Paul sont **les plus** intelligents de la classe.
masc. pl.
Mary and Paul are the most intelligent in the class.

Lowest degree – The superlative of lowest degree is formed as follows: **le, la,** or **les** (depending on the gender and number of the noun described) + **moins** *(less)* + adjective.

Paul est **le moins** actif de la classe.
masc. sing.
Paul is the least active in the classe.

Careful
In English and in French, a few adjectives have irregular forms of comparison which you will have to memorize individually.

adjective	Cette pomme est **bonne.**
	This apple is good.
comparative	Cette pomme est **meilleure.**
	This apple is better.
superlative	Cette pomme est **la meilleure.**
	This apple is the best.

▼▼▼▼▼▼▼▼▼▼▼▼▼▼▼**REVIEW** ▼▼▼▼▼▼▼▼▼▼▼▼▼▼▼▼

I. Underline the superlative and comparative adjectives in the sentences below.
- Draw an arrow from the adjective to the noun it modifies.
- Circle the various degrees of comparison: superlative (S), comparative of greater degree (C+), comparative of equal degree (C=), or comparative of lesser degree (C-).

1. The teacher is older than the students.   S   C+   C=   C-

2. He is less intelligent than I am.   S   C+   C=   C-

3. Mary is as tall as Paul.   S   C+   C=   C-

4. That boy is the worst in the school.   S   C+   C=   C-

5. Paul is a better student than Mary.   S   C+   C=   C-

34. WHAT IS AN ADVERB?

An **adverb** is a word that describes a verb, an adjective, or another adverb. It indicates quantity, time, place, intensity, or manner.[1]

Mary drives *well.*
      | |
   verb adverb

The house is *very* big.
         | |
       adverb adjective

The girl ran *too quickly.*
        | |
     adverb adverb

IN ENGLISH

There are different types of adverbs:

- adverbs of **manner** answer the question *how?* They are the most common adverbs and usually easy to recognize because they end with *-ly*.

   Mary sings *beautifully.*
   Beautifully describes the verb *sings*–it tells you how Mary sings.

   They parked the car *carefully.*
   Carefully describes the verb *parked*–it tells you how the car was parked.

- adverbs of **quantity** or **degree** answer the question *how much?*

   Paul does *well enough* in class.

- adverbs of **time** answer the question *when?*

   He will come *soon.*

- adverbs of **place** answer the question *where?*

   The old were left *behind.*

IN FRENCH

You will have to memorize most adverbs as vocabulary. Most adverbs of manner can be recognized by the ending **-ment** which corresponds to the English ending *-ly*.

---

[1]In English and in French, the structure for comparing adverbs is the same as the structure for comparing adjectives (see **What is Meant by Comparison of Adjectives?**, p. 105).

joliment	beautifully
généralement	generally
heureusement	happily

The most important fact for you to remember is that adverbs are invariable: this means that they never become plural, nor do they have gender.

Adverb or Adjective?

Because adverbs are invariable and adjectives must agree with the noun they modify, you must be able to distinguish one from the other. When you write a sentence in French, always make sure that adjectives agree with the nouns or pronouns they modify and that adverbs remain unchanged.

> *The **tall** girl talked **rapidly**.*
> *Tall* modifies the noun *girl;* it is an adjective. *Rapidly* modifies the verb *talked;* it describes how she talked; it is an adverb.
>
> La **grande** fille parlait **rapidement**.
>   fem. sing.   adverb

> *The **tall** boy talked **rapidly**.*
> *Tall* modifies the noun *boy;* it is an adjective. *Rapidly* modifies the verb *talked;* it describes how he talked; it is an adverb.
>
> Le **grand** garçon parlait **rapidement**.
>   masc. sing.   adverb

Remember that in English *good* is an adjective; *well* is an adverb.

> The student writes *good* English.
> *Good* modifies the noun *English;* it is therefore an adjective.

> The student writes *well*.
> *Well* modifies the verb *writes;* it is therefore an adverb.

Likewise, in French **bon** is an adjective meaning *good;* **bien** is the adverb meaning *well*.

> *The **good** students speak French **well**.*
>   adjective   adverb

> Les **bons** étudiants parlent **bien** le français.
>   masc. pl.   adverb

▼▼▼▼▼▼▼▼▼▼▼▼▼▼REVIEW ▼▼▼▼▼▼▼▼▼▼▼▼▼▼▼▼

Circle the adverbs in the sentences below.
▪ Draw an arrow from the adverb to the word it modifies.

1. The students arrived early.

2. Paul learned the lesson really quickly.

3. The students were too tired to study.

4. He has a reasonably secure income.

5. Mary is a good student who speaks French very well.

35. WHAT IS A CONJUNCTION?

A **conjunction** is a word that links words or groups of words.

IN ENGLISH

There are two kinds of conjunctions: coordinating and subordinating.

Coordinating conjunctions join words, phrases, and clauses that are equal; they *coordinate* elements of equal rank. The major coordinating conjunctions are *and, but, or, nor, for,* and *yet.*

> good *or* evil
> over the river *and* through the woods
> They invited us, *but* we couldn't go.

Subordinating conjunctions join a dependent clause to a main clause; they *subordinate* one clause to another. A clause introduced by a subordinating conjunction is called a **subordinate clause**. Typical subordinating conjunctions are *before, after, since, although, because, if, unless, so that, while, that,* and *when.*

> *Although* we were invited, we didn't go.
> | |___ ___|
> subordinating   main
> conjunction   clause

> They left *because* they were bored.
> |___ ___| |
>   main   subordinating
>   clause   conjunction

> He said *that* he was tired.
> |___ ___| |
>   main   subordinating
>   clause conjunction

Notice that the subordinate clause may come either at the beginning of the sentence or after the main clause.

IN FRENCH

Conjunctions must be memorized as vocabulary items. Remember that, like adverbs and prepositions, conjunctions are invariable (i.e., they never change their form).

▼▼▼▼▼▼▼▼▼▼▼▼▼▼REVIEW ▼▼▼▼▼▼▼▼▼▼▼▼▼▼▼▼

Circle the coordinating and subordinating conjunctions in the sentences below.
■ Underline the words each conjunction serves to coordinate or to subordinate.

1. Mary and Paul were going to study French or Spanish.

2. She did not study because she was too tired.

3. Not only had he forgotten his ticket, but he had forgotten his passport as well.

36. WHAT IS A PREPOSITION?

A **preposition** is a word that shows the relationship of one word (usually a noun or pronoun) to another word in the sentence. The noun or pronoun following the preposition is called the **object of the preposition**. The preposition plus its object is called a **prepositional phrase**.

IN ENGLISH

Prepositions normally indicate position, direction, or time.

- prepositions showing position

    Paul was *in* the car.
    Mary put the books *on* the table.

- prepositions showing direction

    Mary went *to* school.
    The students came directly *from* class.

- preposition showing time

    French people go on vacation *in* August.
    Before class, they went to eat.

Not all prepositions are single words:

because of	in front of	instead of
due to	in spite of	on account of

IN FRENCH

You will have to memorize prepositions as vocabulary. Their meaning and use must be carefully studied. There are two important things to remember:

1. Prepositions are invariable. This means that they never change their form. (They never become plural, nor do they have a gender.)

2. Prepositions are tricky. Every language uses prepositions differently. Do not assume that the same preposition is used in French as in English, or even that a preposition will be used in French when one is used in English (and vice versa).

English	French
Change of preposition	
to be angry *with*	être fâché **contre** *(against)*
to be *on* the plane	être **dans** *(in)* l'avion

Preposition	**No preposition**
to wait *for*	attendre
to look *at*	regarder

No Preposition	**Preposition**
to telephone	téléphoner à
to ask (someone)	demander à

A dictionary will usually give you the verb plus the preposition when one is required.

Careful
Do not translate an English verb + preposition with a word-for-word French equivalent. (See p. 24.)

▼▼▼▼▼▼▼▼▼▼▼▼▼▼REVIEW ▼▼▼▼▼▼▼▼▼▼▼▼▼▼▼▼
Circle the prepositions in the following sentences.

1. The students didn't understand what the lesson was about.

2. His family had come from Paris the year before we had.

3. The teacher walked around the room as she talked.

4. Contrary to popular opinion he was a good student.

5. The garden between the two houses was very small.

37. WHAT ARE OBJECTS?

Every sentence consists, at the very least, of a subject and a verb. This is called the **sentence base.**

Children play.
Work stopped.

The subject of the sentence base is usually a noun or pronoun. Many sentences contain other nouns or pronouns which are related to the action of the verb or to a preposition. These nouns or pronouns are called **objects.**

Paul writes a letter.
subject verb   object

He speaks to Mary.
subject verb   object

Paul goes out with Mary.
subject verb preposition object

We will study the three types of objects separately: direct object, indirect object, and object of a preposition.

Direct Object

IN ENGLISH

A direct object is a noun or pronoun that receives the action of the verb directly, without a preposition between the verb and the following noun or pronoun object. It answers the question *whom?* or *what?* or asked after the verb.[1]

Paul writes *a letter.*
Paul writes what? A letter.
A *letter* is the direct object.

They see *Paul and Mary.*
They see whom? Paul and Mary.
Paul and Mary are the two direct objects.

---

[1] In this section, we will consider active sentences only (see **What is Meant by Active and Passive Voice?**, p. 85.)

Paul sees well.

Paul sees *what?* No answer.
Paul sees *whom?* No answer.

Do not assume that any word which comes right after a verb is automatically the direct object. It must answer the question *what?* or *whom?*

There is no direct object in the sentence. *Well* is an adverb; it answers the question: Paul sees *how?*

Verbs can be classified as to whether or not they take a direct object.

- a **transitive verb** is a verb which takes a direct object. It is indicated by the abbreviation *v.t.* (verb transitive) in dictionaries.

> The boy *threw* the ball.
>   transitive direct object

- an **intransitive verb** is a verb that does not require a direct object. It is indicated by the abbreviation *v.i.* (verb intransitive) in the dictionary.

> Paul *is sleeping.*
>   intransitive

IN FRENCH

As in English, a direct object is a noun or pronoun that receives the action of the verb directly, without a preposition. It answers the question **qui?** *(whom?)* or **quoi?** *(what?)* asked after the verb.

> Ils rencontrent **Paul et Marie.**
> No preposition separates "Paul et Marie"
> from the verb "rencontrent."
> *They meet **Paul and Mary.***

> Paul prend **le livre.**
> No preposition separates "le livre"
> from the verb "prend."
> *Paul takes **the book.***

As with English verbs, French verbs can be transitive or intransitive depending on whether or not they are followed by a direct object.

Indirect Object

IN ENGLISH

An indirect object is a noun or pronoun which receives the action of the verb indirectly, with the preposition *to* relating it to the verb. It answers the question *to whom?* or *to what?* asked after the verb.

> She spoke *to her friends.*
> She spoke to whom? Her friends.
> *Her friends* is the indirect object.

> He gave the painting *to the museum.*
> He gave a painting to what? The museum.
> *The museum* is the indirect object.

IN FRENCH

As in English, an indirect object is a noun or pronoun which receives the action of the verb indirectly, with the preposition **à** *(to)* relating it to the verb. It answers the question **à qui?** *(to whom?)* or **à quoi** *(to what?)* asked after the verb. Nouns that are indirect objects are easy to identify in French because they are always preceded by the preposition **à.**

> Paul parle **à son frère.**
> *Paul speaks **to his brother.***

> Il pense **à l'examen.**
> *He is thinking **about the exam.***

Sentences With a Direct and Indirect Object

A sentence may contain both a direct object and an indirect object.

IN ENGLISH

When a sentence has both a direct and an indirect object, the following two word orders are possible:

1. subject (S) + verb (V) + indirect object (IO) + direct object (DO)

> Paul gave his sister a gift.
> S   V   IO   DO

> *Who* gave a gift? Paul.
> *Paul* is the subject.

> Paul gave *what?* A gift.
> *A gift* is the direct object.

Paul gave a gift *to whom?* His sister.
His sister is the indirect object.

2. subject + verb + direct object + *to* + indirect object

    Paul gave a gift to his sister
    S   V   DO   IO

The first structure, under 1, is the most common. However, because there is no *"to"* preceding the indirect object, it is more difficult to identify its function than in the second structure. Be sure to ask the questions to establish the function of words in a sentence.

IN FRENCH
There is only one word order possible when a sentence contains both a direct and an indirect object noun (pronoun objects follow a different word order): subject + verb + direct object + à + indirect object

    Paul a donné un cadeau à sa soeur.
    S   V   DO   IO

*Paul gave **his sister a gift**.*
*Paul gave **a gift to his sister**.*

Object of a Preposition

IN ENGLISH
An object of a preposition is a noun or pronoun that receives the action of the verb through a preposition other than *to*. (Objects of the preposition *to* are discussed under indirect objects above.) It answers the question *whom?* or *what?* asked after the preposition.

    Paul works *for Mary.*
    Paul works *for whom*? For Mary.
    Mary is the object of the preposition *for.*

    The baby eats *with a spoon.*
    The baby eats *with what*? With a spoon.
    A spoon is the object of the preposition *with.*

IN FRENCH
An object of a preposition is a noun or pronoun that receives the action of the verb through a preposition other than à *(to)*. It answers the question **qui?** *(whom?)* or **quoi?** *(what?)* asked after the preposition.

Paul travaille **pour Marie.**
Paul works for Mary.

Le bébé mange **avec une cuillère.**
The baby eats with a spoon.

Careful

The relationship between a verb and its object is often different in English and French. For example, a verb may take an object of a preposition in English but a direct object in French, or a direct object in English but an indirect object in French. For this reason, it is important that you pay close attention to such differences when you learn French verbs. Your textbook, as well as dictionaries, will indicate when a French verb needs a preposition before an object (see p. 24).

Here are some of the differences that you are likely to encounter.

1. object of a preposition in English → direct object in French

> *I am looking for the book.*
> Function in English: Object of a preposition
> I am looking *for what*? The book.
> *The book* is the object of the preposition *for.*

> Je cherche **le livre.**
> Function in French: Direct object
> Je cherche *quoi*? Le livre.
> **Le livre** is a direct object since **chercher** is not followed by a preposition.

Many common verbs require an indirect object or an object of a preposition in English but a direct object in French.

to listen **to**	écouter
to look **at**	regarder
to wait **for**	attendre
to pay **for**	payer

2. direct object in English → indirect object in French

> *She phones her friends every day.*
> Function in English: Direct object
> She phones *whom*? Her friends.
> *Her friends* is the direct object.

Elle téléphone **à ses amis** tous les jours.
Function in French: Indirect object
Elle téléphone **à qui?** A ses amis.
The verb is **téléphoner à** and takes an indirect object.

A few common verbs require a direct object in English and an indirect object in French.

to obey   obéir **à**
to resemble   ressembler **à**

3. direct object in English → object of a preposition in French

*Mary's parents remember **the war**.*
Function in English: Direct object
Mary's parents remember *what?* The war.
The war is the direct object.

Les parents de Marie se souviennent **de la guerre**.
Function in French: Object of preposition
Les parents de Marie se souviennent **de quoi?** De la guerre.
The verb is **se souvenir de** and it requires an object for the preposition **de**.

Here is another common verb which requires a direct object in English and an object of a preposition in French.

to enter   entrer **dans**

Always identify the function of a word within the language in which you are working; do not mix English patterns into French.

Summary

The different types of objects in a sentence can be identified by looking to see if they are introduced by a preposition and, if so, by which one.

Direct object – An object which receives the action of the verb directly, without a preposition.

Indirect object - An object which receives the action of the verb indirectly, through the preposition *to.*

Object of a preposition – An object which receives the action of the verb through a preposition other than *to.*

Your ability to recognize the three types of objects is essential. With pronouns, for instance, a different French pronoun is used for the English pronoun *him* depending on whether *him* is a direct object (**le**) or an indirect object (**lui**).

▼▼▼▼▼▼▼▼▼▼▼▼▼▼**REVIEW** ▼▼▼▼▼▼▼▼▼▼▼▼▼▼▼▼

Find the objects in the sentences below:
- Next to Q, write the question you need to ask to find the object.
- Next to A, write the answer to the question you just asked.
- Circle the kind of object it is: direct object (DO), indirect object (IO) or object of a preposition (OP).

1. The children took a shower.

Q: _____

A: _____   DO   IO   OP

2. They ate the meal with their friends.

Q: _____

A: _____   DO   IO   OP

Q: _____

A: _____   DO   IO   OP

3. He sent a present to his brother.

Q: _____

A: _____   DO   IO   OP

Q: _____

A: _____   DO   IO   OP

38. WHAT IS AN OBJECT PRONOUN?

An **object pronoun** is a pronoun used as an object of a verb or a preposition.

IN ENGLISH

Pronouns change according to their function in the sentence. Pronouns used as subjects are studied in **What is a Subject Pronoun?**, p. 32. We use subject pronouns when we conjugate verbs (see **What is a Verb Conjugation?**, p. 36). Object pronouns are used when a pronoun is either a direct object, indirect object, or object of a preposition. (See **What are Objects?**, p. 116.)

The form of the object pronoun is different from the form of the subject pronoun, but the same form pronoun is used as a direct object, indirect object, or an object of a preposition.

	Subject	Object
Singular		
1st person	I	me
2nd person	you	you
3rd person	{ he	him
	she	her
	it	it
Plural		
1st person	we	us
2nd person	you	you
3rd person	they	them

She saw *me*.
　　　direct object → object pronoun

I lent my car to *him*.
　　　indirect object → object pronoun

They went out with *her*.
　　　object of a preposition → object pronoun

In English, the object pronoun is always placed after the verb.

IN FRENCH

As in English, the pronouns used as subjects are different from the ones used as objects. Unlike English, however, in many cases a different object pronoun is used for each kind of object: direct, indirect, and object of a preposition. You will therefore have to learn how to analyze the function of an object pronoun so that you can choose the correct French form.

In French, the object pronouns are usually placed before the verb. Consult your textbook for the rules.

French Direct Object Pronouns

First, you have to establish that the French verb takes a direct object. Remember that English and French verbs don't always take the same type of objects and that when working in French you will have to establish the type of object taken by the French verb (see p. 120).

Let us look at the French direct object pronouns to see how they are selected. Since the rules for the selection of 1st and 2nd person direct object pronouns are different from the rules for the selection of 3rd person direct object pronouns, we have divided the French direct object pronouns into these two categories:

1st and 2nd Persons Singular and Plural (me, you, and us)
The direct object pronoun of the 1st or 2nd person are merely a question of memorization. Select the form you need from the chart below and place it before the verb.

	Subject	Direct object
Singular		
1st person	je	**me**
2nd person	tu	**te**
Plural		
1st person	nous	**nous**
2nd person	vous	**vous**

To simplify our examples, we have chosen a verb which takes a direct object both in English and in French, the verb *to see* (**voir**).

*Paul sees **you**.*
1. Identify the verb: to see
2. What is the French equivalent: **voir**
3. Does the French verb require a preposition before an object: No.
4. Function of pronoun in French: direct object
5. Selection: **te** or **vous**

Paul **te** voit.
Paul **vous** voit.

The fact that **nous** and **vous** can be either the subject or the object in a sentence is sometimes confusing, particularly since both subject and object pronouns are placed before the verb in French. It is important that you do not think of **nous** and **vous** only as subjects. In case of doubt, look at the verb. Remember that verbs agree with their subject. If **nous** is the subject, the verb will end in **-ons**; if it doesn't, **nous** is an object of some kind. The same is true with **vous**. If it is the subject of the verb, the ending of regular verbs will be **-ez**.

Vous **nous** voyez tous les jours.
Nous cannot be the subject because the verb **voir** doesn't end in **-ons**. The subject of **voyez** can only be **vous**. Therefore, **nous** must be an object pronoun.
*You see **us** everyday.*

3rd Person Singular and Plural (him, her, it and them)
The French direct objects of the 3rd person have a different form depending on the gender and number of the pronoun.

	Subject	Direct object
Singular		
masculine	il	**le**
feminine	elle	**la**
Plural		
masculine	ils	**les**
feminine	elles	**les**

An analysis of the following sentences, in which we have used each of the 3rd person direct object pronouns, will enable us to select the proper French form from the chart above. We have again used the verb **to see** *(voir)* because both the English and the French verbs take a direct object.

HIM - Always masculine singular.

*Do you see Paul? Yes, I see **him.***
Voyez-vous Paul? Oui, je **le** vois.

HER - Always feminine singular.

*Do you see Mary? Yes, I see **her.***
Voyez-vous Marie? Oui, je **la** vois.

IT - Always singular, but the gender will depend on the gender of the noun it refers to (its antecedent).

*Do you see the book? Yes, I see **it.***
Voyez-vous le livre? Oui, je **le** vois.
   1. Antecedent: **Le livre** *(the book)* is masculine.
   2. Gender: masculine
   3. Selection: **le**

*Do you see the table? Yes, I see **it.***
Voyez-vous la table? Oui, je **la** vois.
   1. Antecedent: **La table** *(the table)* is feminine.
   2. Gender: feminine
   3. Selection: **la**

THEM - Always plural and the same form is used for both genders.

*Do you see the girls? Yes, I see **them.***
Voyez-vous les jeunes filles? Oui, je **les** vois.

*Do you see the boys? Yes, I see **them.***
Voyez-vous les garçons? Oui, je **les** vois.

French Indirect Object Pronouns

First, you have to establish that the French verb takes an indirect object. Remember that English and French verbs don't always take the same type of objects and that when working in French you will have to establish the type of object taken by the French verb (see p. 120).

In French it is easier to distinguish between direct and indirect objects with nouns rather than with pronouns because nouns that are indirect objects are always preceded by the preposition **à** whereas indirect object pronouns are not.

Let us look at the French indirect object pronouns to see how they are selected. Since the rules for the selection of 1st and 2nd persons indirect object pronouns are different from the rules for the selection of 3rd person indirect object pronouns, we have divided the French indirect object pronouns into these two categories:

1st and 2nd Persons Singular and Plural (me, you, and us)
The indirect object pronoun of the 1st and 2nd persons is the same as the direct object pronoun. Select the form you need from the chart below.

	Subject	Direct and indirect objects
Singular		
1st person	je	**me**
2nd person	tu	**te**
Plural		
1st person	nous	**nous**
2nd person	vous	**vous**

To simplify our examples, we have chosen a verb which takes an indirect object both in English and in French, the verb *to speak to* (**parler à**).

> *Paul speaks **to us**.*
> 1. Identify the verb: to speak
> 2. What is the French equivalent: **parler**
> 3. Is the French verb followed by à: Yes.
> 4. Function of the pronoun in French: indirect object

> Paul **nous** parle.
> |
> indirect object pronoun

3rd Person Singular and Plural (him, her, it and them)
Since the rules for the selection of 3rd person indirect object pronouns are different for pronouns referring to a "person" (this category includes human beings and live animals) and pronouns referring to a "thing" (this category includes objects and ideas), we have divided 3rd person pronouns into these two categories.

"Person" – antecedent is a person (*him, her,* and *them*)
There are two forms of the indirect object pronoun, a singular and a plural form.

	Direct object	Indirect object
Singular		
masculine	le	**lui**
feminine	la	**lui**
Plural		
masculine	les	**leur**
feminine	les	**leur**

HIM OR HER - Always singular.

> *Are you speaking to Paul? Yes, I am speaking **to him**.*
> 1. Identify the verb: to speak
> 2. What is the French equivalent: **parler**
> 3. Does the French verb require a preposition before an object? Yes.
> 4. What preposition? **à**
> 5. Function of the pronoun in French: indirect object
> 6. Selection: **lui**

Parlez-vous à Paul? Oui, je **lui** parle.

> *Are you speaking to Mary? Yes, I am speaking **to her**.*
> 1 - 6. See above.

Parlez-vous à Marie? Oui, je **lui** parle.

The only way you can tell if **lui** refers to a male or female is from what has been said before.

THEM – Always plural. You will have to determine whether the noun it refers to (its antecedent) is a person or a thing. If it refers to a person, always use the indirect object pronoun **leur.**

> *Are you speaking to Paul and Mary? Yes, I am speaking **to them**.*
> 1 - 5. See above.
> 6. Type of antecedent: person (Paul and Mary)
> 7. Selection: **leur**

Parlez-vous à Paul et à Marie? Oui, je **leur** parle.

"Thing" – antecedent is a thing (*it* and *them*)
There is only one form of the indirect object pronoun **y**.

Antecedent:	Direct Object	Indirect Object Person	Thing
Singular			
masculine	le	lui	y
feminine	la	lui	y
Plural			
masculine	les	leur	y
feminine	les	leur	y

Are you answering the letter? Yes, I am answering **it.**
    1. Identify the verb: to answer
    2. What is the French equivalent: **répondre**
    3. Does the French verb require a preposition before an object? Yes
    4. What preposition? **à**
    5. Function of pronoun in French: indirect object
    6. Type of antecedent: thing *(the letter)*
    7. Selection: **y**
Répondez-vous **à la lettre**? Oui, j'**y** réponds.

Do you obey the laws? Yes, I obey **them.**
    1. Identify the verb: to obey
    2. What is the French equivalent: **obéir**
    3. Does the French verb require a preposition before an object: Yes
    4. What preposition: **à**
    5. Function of pronoun in French: indirect object
    6. Type of antecedent: thing *(the laws)*
    7. Selection: **y**
Obéissez-vous **aux** lois? Oui, j'**y** obéis.
        à + les

French Pronouns as Objects of a Preposition

First, you have to establish that the French verb takes an object of a preposition. Remember that English and French verbs don't always take the same type of objects and that when working in French you will have to establish the type of object taken by the French verb (see p. 120).

Pronouns that are objects of prepositions other than *to* (**à** in French) have certain forms which are different from the forms used as direct objects and indirect objects. Unlike other object pronouns which are usually placed before the verb, pronouns as objects of prepositions are usually placed, with the preposition, after the verb. In this they are like nouns used as objects of prepositions. (The pronoun **en** is an exception to this rule, see below under 2.)

Let us look at the French pronouns objects of a preposition to see how they are selected. Because the rules for the selection of objects of a preposition pronouns of the 1st and 2nd persons are different from the rules for the selection of the object of a preposition pronoun of the 3rd person, we have divided the French object of a preposition pronouns into these two categories:

1st and 2nd Person Singular and Plural (me, you, and us)
The 1st and 2nd person object of a preposition pronouns are merely a question of memorization. Select the form you need from the chart below and place it, with the preposition, after the verb.

	Subject	Direct & indirect object	Object of preposition
Singular			
1st person	je	me	prép. + **moi**
2nd person	tu	te	prép. + **toi**
Plural			
1st person	nous	nous	prép. + **nous**
2nd person	vous	vous	prép. + **vous**

Here is an example.

Is the book for Paul ?   *No, it's for **me**.*
*No, it's for **you**.*
*No, it's for **us**.*

    1. Identify the verb: to be
    2. What is the French equivalent: **être**
    3. Is the French verb followed by a preposition? Yes.
    4. What preposition? **pour** *(for)*
    5. Function of pronoun in French: object of preposition
    6. Selection: **moi, toi (vous), nous**
Est-ce que le livre est pour Paul? Non, il est pour **moi**.
                                    Non, il est pour **toi** *(or* vous*)*.
                                    Non, il est pour **nous**.

3rd Person Singular and Plural (him, her, it and them)

Since the rules for the selection of 3rd person object of a preposition pronouns are different for pronouns referring to a "person" (this category includes human beings and live animals) and pronouns referring to a "thing" (this category includes objects and ideas), we have divided 3rd person pronouns into these two categories.

"Person" – antecedent is a person (*him, her* and *them*)

There are four forms of the object of preposition pronouns referring to a person depending on the gender and number of the pronoun.

Antecedent	Subject	Direct object	Indirect object	Object of preposition
	Person & Thing		Person	Person
Singular				
masculine	il	le	lui	prép. + **lui**
feminine	elle	la	lui	prép. + **elle**
Plural				
masculine	ils	les	leur	prép. + **eux**
feminine	elles	les	leur	prép. + **eux**

An analysis of the following sentences, in which we have used each of the 3rd person pronouns object of a preposition referring to persons, will enable us to select the proper French form from the chart above.

HIM – Always masculine singular.

*Is the book for Paul ? Yes, it is for **him**.*
1. Identify the verb: to be
2. What is the French equivalent: **être**
3. Is the French verb followed by a preposition? Yes.
4. What preposition? **pour** *(for)*
5. Function of pronoun in French: object of preposition
6. Gender of antecedent: masculine *(Paul)*
7. Selection: **lui**

Est-ce que le livre est pour Paul? Oui, il est pour **lui**.

HER – Always feminine singular.

*Is the book for Mary? Yes, it is for **her**.*
1 - 5. See above.
6. Gender of antecedent: feminine (Mary)
7. Selection: **elle**

Est-ce que le livre est pour Marie? Oui, il est pour **elle**.

THEM — Always plural. You will have to determine whether the noun it refers to is a person or a thing. A different object pronoun is used if the antecedent is a person or thing. If the antecedent is a person, you will have to determine the gender of the antecedent.

*Is the book for the girls? Yes it is for **them**.*
1 - 5. See above.
6. Gender of antecedent: feminine *(the girls)*
7. Selection: **elles**
Est-ce que le livre est pour les filles? Oui, il est pour **elles**.

*Is the book for the boys? Yes it is for **them**.*
1 - 5. See above.
6. Gender of antecedent: masculine *(the boys)*
7. Selection: **eux**
Est-ce que le livre est pour les garçons? Oui, il est pour **eux**.

"Thing" – antecedent is a thing *(it* and *them)*
In French, a noun referring to a thing is only replaced by a pronoun when it is the object of the preposition **de**. (A noun referring to a thing preceded by any other preposition is not replaced. For instance, in French you cannot say "The book is on *it*" referring to *the table*; instead one says "The book is on *the table*.") When *it* or *them* is the object of the preposition **de,** both the preposition and the pronoun are replaced by **en** which is placed before the verb.[1]

	Subject	Direct objects	Indirect object		Object of preposition	
Antecedent	**Person & Thing**		**Person**	**Thing**	**Person**	**Thing** (after de)
Singular						
masculine	il	le	lui	y	lui	en
feminine	elle	la	lui	y	elle	en
Plural						
masculine	ils	les	leur	y	eux	en
feminine	elles	les	leur	y	elles	en

---

[1]Your textbook may cover the few cases in which the pronoun en can be used to refer to persons.

Here are some examples:

*I liked the book so l am going to speak **about it**.*
1. Identify the verb: to speak
2. What is the French equivalent: **parler**
3. Is the French verb followed by **de**: Yes
4. Function of pronoun in French: object of preposition **de**
5. Type of antecedent: thing *(book)*
6. Selection: **en**

J'ai aimé le livre alors je vais **en** parler.

*I liked these books so l am going to speak **about them**.*
1 - 6. See above.

J'ai aimé ces livres alors je vais **en** parler.

Disjunctive (Stressed) Pronouns

The set of pronouns used as objects of prepositions has another function. These pronouns, without the preposition, are also used for emphasis or contrast. In this function, they are called **disjunctive** or **stressed pronouns**. Disjunctive pronouns often stand alone.

*Who is there? **Him**.*
                ***Her**.*
                     |
        personal pronoun standing alone

Qui est là? **Lui.**
            Elle.
                |
        disjunctive pronoun

*Who called? **Me**.*
            |
   personal pronoun standing alone

Qui a téléphoné? **Moi.**
                    |
        disjunctive pronoun

Summary

Below is a flow chart of the steps you have to follow to find the French equivalent of each English object pronoun. It is important that you do the steps in sequence, because each step depends on the previous one.

DO → Direct object in the French sentence

IO → Indirect object in the French sentence

OP → Object of a preposition or disjunctive pronoun in the French sentence

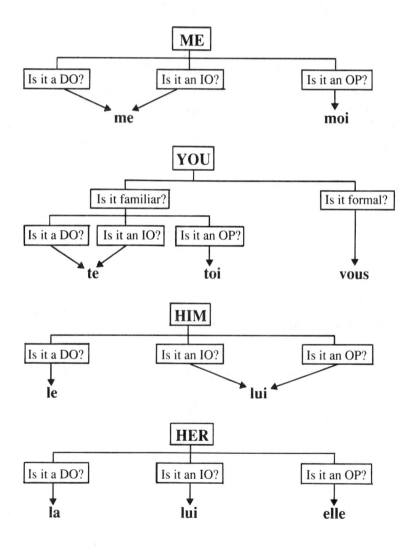

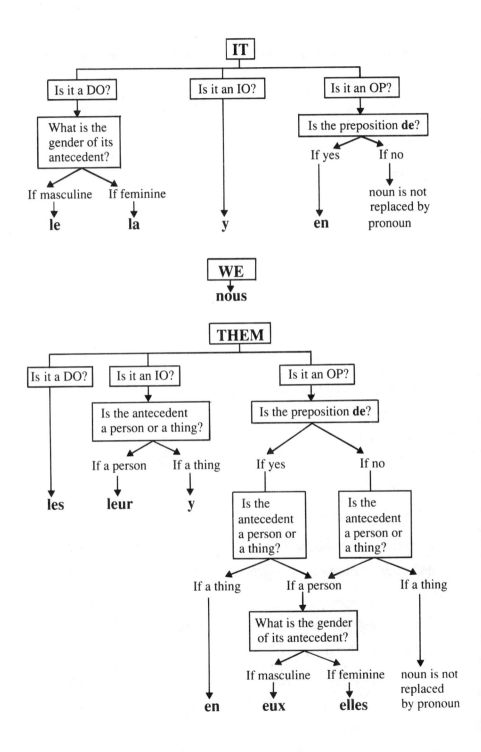

▼▼▼▼▼▼▼▼▼▼▼▼▼▼REVIEW ▼▼▼▼▼▼▼▼▼▼▼▼▼▼▼▼
Underline the object pronoun in the sentences below.
- Using the chart on pp. 134-35, circle the correct French equivalent: direct object (DO), indirect object (IO) or object of a preposition (OP), person (P), or thing (T)

1. Mary likes the book and she takes it.

   to take → **prendre**

FUNCTION OF PRONOUN IN ENGLISH:	DO	IO	OP
FUNCTION OF PRONOUN IN FRENCH:	DO	IO	OP
ANTECEDENT IN ENGLISH: _____			
GENDER OF ANTECEDENT IN FRENCH: masculine			

   Marie aime le livre et elle_____prend.

2. The teacher spoke to them about the exam yesterday.

   to speak to → **parler à**

FUNCTION OF PRONOUN IN ENGLISH:	DO	IO	OP
FUNCTION OF PRONOUN IN FRENCH:	DO	IO	OP
TYPE OF ANTECEDENT:	P	T	

   Le professeur_____a parlé de l'examen hier.

3. Go with her.

   to go with → **aller avec**

FUNCTION OF PRONOUN IN ENGLISH:	DO	IO	OP
FUNCTION OF PRONOUN IN FRENCH:	DO	IO	OP

   Va avec_____

4. Is the present for your parents? Yes, it's for them.

   to be for → **être pour**

FUNCTION OF PRONOUN IN ENGLISH:	DO	IO	OP
FUNCTION OF PRONOUN IN FRENCH:	DO	IO	OP

IS IT THE OBJECT OF PREPOSITION DE: YES   NO

ANTECEDENT IN ENGLISH: _____

TYPE OF ANTECEDENT: P   T

GENDER ANTECEDENT IN FRENCH: masculine

Le cadeau est-il pour tes parents? Oui, il est pour _____

5. Did you answer his letters? No, we will answer them today.

to answer → **répondre à**

FUNCTION OF PRONOUN IN ENGLISH: DO   IO   OP

FUNCTION OF PRONOUN IN FRENCH: DO   IO   OP

ANTECEDENT IN ENGLISH: _____

TYPE OF ANTECEDENT: P   T

Avez-vous répondu à ses lettres? Non, nous_____répondrons

aujourd'hui.

6. Paul doesn't like exams. He is afraid of them.

to be afraid of → **avoir peur de**

FUNCTION OF PRONOUN IN ENGLISH: DO   IO   OP

FUNCTION OF PRONOUN IN FRENCH: DO   IO   OP

IS IT THE OBJECT OF PREPOSITION DE: YES   NO

ANTECEDENT IN ENGLISH: _____

TYPE OF ANTECEDENT: P   T

Paul n'aime pas les examens. Il_____a peur.

39. WHAT IS AN INTERROGATIVE PRONOUN?

An **Interrogative pronoun** is a word that replaces a noun and introduces a question. Interrogative comes from *interrogate*, to question.

IN ENGLISH
Different interrogative pronouns are used depending on whether you are referring to a "person" (this category includes human beings and live animals) or a "thing" (this category includes objects and ideas). Also, the form of the interrogative pronoun referring to persons changes according to its function in the sentence.

IN FRENCH
A different interrogative pronoun is used depending on whether the pronoun replaces a person or a thing. Also, the interrogative pronoun changes according to its function in the sentence.

In English and in French, an interrogative pronoun can be a subject, a direct object, an indirect object, or an object of a preposition. We shall study each type separately.

Subject

IN ENGLISH
An interrogative subject pronoun is always followed directly by the verb. A different interrogative pronoun is used depending on whether the subject interrogative pronoun refers to a person or a thing.

"Person"
Who is used for the subject of the sentence.

> *Who* speaks French?
> subject verb

"Thing"
What is used for the subject of the sentence.

> *What* is on the table?
> subject verb

IN FRENCH
As in English, an interrogative subject pronoun is always followed directly by a verb. Also, a different interrogative pronoun is used depending on whether the subject interrogative pronoun refers to a person or a thing.

"Person"
Qui + verb *or* Qui est-ce qui + verb are interchangeable.

> Qui parle français?
> Qui est-ce qui parle français?
> └────┬────┘ |
>   subject   verb
> *Who speaks French?*
> |
> subject of *speaks*

"Thing"
Qu'est-ce qui + verb is the only form.

> Qu'est-ce qui est sur la table?
> └──────┬──────┘ |
>   subject   verb
> *What is on the table?*
> |
> subject of *is*

Direct Object

IN ENGLISH
A different interrogative pronoun is used depending on whether the direct object interrogative pronoun refers to a person or a thing.

"Person"
Whom is used for the object of the sentence.

> *Whom* do you know here?
> |
> direct object
> *(You* is the subject.)

Because in conversational English *who* is often used instead of *whom* (ex: *"Who* do you know here?"), it is difficult to recognize the interrogative adjective as a direct object. Make sure that you analyze the sentence to establish the function of the interrogative pronoun.

"Thing"
What is used for the object of the sentence.

What do you want?
|
direct object

IN FRENCH
As in English, a different interrogative pronoun is used depending on whether the direct object interrogative pronoun refers to a person or a thing.

"Person"
Qui est-ce que + subject + verb *or* **Qui** + verb + subject are interchangeable. Notice that the form with **"est-ce que"** takes the normal word order, subject + verb, whereas the other form takes an inversion, namely, verb + subject. (See **What are Declarative and Interrogative Sentences?, p. 46.**)

Qui est-ce que vous voyez?
‾‾‾‾‾‾‾
subject + verb

Qui voyez-vous?
‾‾‾‾‾‾
verb + subject
Who(m) do you see?
|
direct object of see
(*You* is the subject.)

"Thing"
Qu'est-ce que + subject + verb *or* **Que** + verb + subject are interchangeable. Notice that the form with **"est-ce que"** takes the normal word order, subject + verb, whereas the other form takes an inversion, namely, verb + subject.)

Qu'est-ce que vous voulez?
‾‾‾‾‾‾
subject + verb

Que voulez-vous?
‾‾‾‾‾
verb + subject
What do you want?
|
direct object of want
(*You* is the subject.)

Indirect Object and Object of a Preposition

IN ENGLISH
There is no difference between the form of the interrogative pronoun as an indirect object or as an object of a preposition. However, a different interrogative pronoun is used depending on whether it refers to a person or a thing. When it serves as an indirect object, it is preceded by the preposition *to;* if it is preceded by any other preposition, it is considered an object of a preposition.

It is often difficult to identify the function of a pronoun because, in English, a preposition is often placed at the end of the sentence, separated from the interrogative pronoun to which it is linked. This separation of a preposition from its object is called a **dangling preposition**.

Who did you speak *to?*
interr. pronoun   preposition

Who did you get the book *from?*
interr. pronoun   preposition

To make it easier for you to identify indirect object pronouns and object of a preposition pronouns, you will have to change the structure of the sentence so that the preposition is placed before the pronoun. This restructuring will not only make it easier for you to identify the function of the pronoun, but it will also establish the word order for the French sentence.

The following sentences have been restructured to avoid a dangling preposition.

Who are you giving the book *to?*
pronoun   preposition
To whom are you giving the book?
indirect object

What are you contributing *to?*
pronoun   preposition
To what are you contributing?
indirect object

Who are you going out *with?*
pronoun   preposition
With whom are you going out?
object of the preposition *with*

What are you writing *with?*
pronoun   preposition
With what are you writing?
object of the preposition *with*

"Person"
Who (whom) is used for indirect objects and objects of a preposition.

Who did you speak *to?* (*To whom* did you speak?)
indirect object

Who did you get the book *from?* (*From whom* did you get the book?)
object of preposition *from*

"Thing"
What is used for indirect objects and objects of a preposition.

What do you cook *with?* (*With what* do you cook?)
object of preposition *with*

IN FRENCH
As in English, there is no difference between the form of the interrogative pronoun as an indirect object or as an object of a preposition. Also, as in English, a different interrogative pronoun is used depending on whether it refers to a person or a thing. When the interrogative pronoun serves as an indirect object, it is preceded by the preposition à *(to);* if it is preceded by any other preposition, it is considered an object of a preposition.

"Person"

The preposition + **qui** + **est-ce que** + subject + verb *or* preposition + **qui** + verb + subject are interchangeable.

A qui est-ce que vous donnez le livre?

subject + verb

A qui donnez-vous le livre?

verb + subject

To whom are you giving the book?

indirect object
(Book is the direct object.)

Avec qui est-ce que vous sortez?

subject + verb

Avec qui sortez-vous?

verb + subject

With whom are you going out?

object of preposition *with*

"Thing"

The preposition + **quoi** + **est-ce que** + subject + verb *or* preposition + **quoi** + verb + subject are interchangeable.

A quoi est-ce que vous contribuez?

subject + verb

A quoi contribuez-vous?

verb + subject

To what are you contributing?

indirect object

Avec quoi est-ce que vous écrivez?

subject + verb

Avec quoi écrivez-vous?

verb + subject

With what are you writing?

object of the preposition *with*

Careful

Once again we remind you that some French verbs take direct objects, while the equivalent English verbs take an indirect object and vice-versa (see p. 120). Make sure that you determine the function of the pronoun in French.

Summary

To choose the correct form, proceed with the following three steps:

1. Determine the function of the interrogative pronoun in the French sentence (subject, direct object, indirect object, or object of a preposition).

2. Establish whether the pronoun refers to a person or a thing.

3. Refer to the chart below.

	Subject *who*	Direct object *who(m)*	Indirect object and object of a prepositon preposition + *who(m)*
person	qui est-ce qui qui	qui est-ce que qui (+ inversion)	prép. + qui est-ce que prép. + qui (+ inversion)
	what	*what*	preposition + *what*
thing	qu'est-ce qui	qu'est-ce que que (+ inversion)	prép. + quoi est-ce-que prép. + quoi (+ inversion)

"Which one, which ones"

There is another interrogative pronoun which we will now examine separately because it does not follow the same pattern as the ones above.

IN ENGLISH

Which one, which ones can refer to both persons and things; they are used in questions that request the selection of one *(which one,* singular) or more than one *(which ones,* plural) from a group that has already been mentioned. The words *one* and *ones* are often omitted. These interrogative pronouns may be used as a subject, direct object, indirect object, and object of a preposition.

All the teachers are here. *Which one* teaches French?
group mentioned   singular subject

I have two cars. *Which one* do you want to take?
group mentioned   singular direct object

The library has many books. *Which ones* do you want to read?
group mentioned   plural direct object

IN FRENCH

These interrogative pronouns do not change according to their function. They change according to the gender of their antecedent, and their number depends on whether you want to say *which one* (singular) or *which ones* (plural).

	Singular	**Plural**
masculine	lequel	lesquels
feminine	laquelle	lesquelles

To choose the proper form, follow these steps:

1. Determine the antecedent.
2. Determine the gender of the antecedent.
3. Do you wish to say *which one* → singular or *which ones* → plural?
4. Select the correct French form from the above chart.

Let us apply these steps to some examples.

All the teachers are here. **Which one** *teaches French?*
Tous les professeurs sont ici. **Lequel** enseigne le français?
1. Antecedent: the teachers
2. Gender: **Un professeur** *(a professor)* is masculine.
3. Number: *One* is singular.
4. Selection: **lequel**

I have two cars. **Which one** *do you want to take?*
J'ai deux voitures. **Laquelle** veux-tu prendre?
1. Antecedent: the cars
2. Gender: **Une voiture** *(a car)* is feminine.
3. Number: *One* is singular.
4. Selection: **laquelle**

The library has many books. **Which ones** *do you want to read?*
La bibliothèque a beaucoup de livres. **Lesquels** veux-tu lire?
1. Antecedent: books
2. Gender: **Les livres** *(the books)* is masculine.
3. Number: *Ones* is plural.
4. Selection: **lesquels**

Here are four girls; **which ones** *do you want to speak* **to?**
RESTRUCTURE: Place the preposition before the interrogative pronoun.
Here are four girls; **to which ones** *do you want to speak?*
Voici quatre filles; **auxquelles** voulez-vous parler?

à + lesquelles —→ auxquelles

1. Antecedent: girls
2. Gender: **Une fille** *(a girl)* is feminine.
3. Number: *Ones* is plural.
4. Selection: **lesquelles**

There are two books. **Which one** *are you speaking* **about?**
RESTRUCTURE: Place the preposition before the interrogative pronoun.
There are two books. **About which one** *are you speaking?*
Il y a deux livres. **Duquel** parlez-vous?

de + lequel —→ duquel

1. Antecedent: books
2. Gender: **Un livre** *(a book)* is masculine.
3. Number: *One* is singular.
4. Selection: **lequel**

▼▼▼▼▼▼▼▼▼▼▼▼▼▼REVIEW ▼▼▼▼▼▼▼▼▼▼▼▼▼▼▼▼

Underline the interrogative pronouns in the questions below.
▪ Using the chart on p. 144, circle the correct French equivalent: subject (S)
direct object (DO), indirect object (IO) or object of a preposition (OP).

1. Who came into the room?

FUNCTION OF PRONOUN IN ENGLISH:	S	DO	IO	OP
FUNCTION OF PRONOUN IN FRENCH:	S	DO	IO	OP

_____ est entré dans la pièce?

2. Who did you speak to?

RESTRUCTURE: _____

to speak to → **parler à**

FUNCTION OF PRONOUN IN ENGLISH:	S	DO	IO	OP
FUNCTION OF PRONOUN IN FRENCH:	S	DO	IO	OP

_____ est-ce que vous avez parlé?

3. What is she doing tonight?

to do → **faire**

FUNCTION OF PRONOUN IN ENGLISH:	S	DO	IO	OP
FUNCTION OF PRONOUN IN FRENCH:	S	DO	IO	OP

_____fait-elle ce soir?

4. Who are you calling?

RESTRUCTURE: _____

to call → **téléphoner à**

FUNCTION OF PRONOUN IN ENGLISH:	S	DO	IO	OP
FUNCTION OF PRONOUN IN FRENCH:	S	DO	IO	OP

_____téléphonez-vous?

40. WHAT IS A POSSESSIVE PRONOUN?

A **possessive pronoun** is a word that replaces a noun and indicates the possessor of that noun. Possessive comes from *possess, to own.*

> Whose house is that? It's *mine.*

Mine is a pronoun that replaces the words *my house* and shows who possesses the house.

IN ENGLISH
Here is a list of the possessive pronouns:

Singular possessor

1st person		mine
2nd person		yours
3rd person	masculine	his
	feminine	hers
	neuter	its

Plural possessor

1st person	ours
2nd person	yours
3rd person	theirs

Possessive pronouns never change their form, regardless of the thing possessed; they only refer to the possessor.

> Is that your house? Yes, it is *mine.*
> Are those your keys? Yes, they are *mine.*

The same possessive pronoun *(mine)* is used, although the objects possessed are different in number *(house* is singular, *keys* is plural).

> John's car is blue. *His* is blue.
> Mary's car is blue. *Hers* is blue.

Although the object possessed is the same *(car),* the possessive pronoun is different because the possessor is different *(John* masculine singular, *Mary* feminine singular).

IN FRENCH
Like English, a French possessive pronoun refers to the possessor, but unlike English, it must agree, like all French pronouns, in gender and number with its antecedent, that is, with the person or object possessed. In addition, the possessive pronoun is preceded by a definite article which also agrees in gender and number with the object pos-

sessed. Therefore, there are masculine and feminine forms in both the singular and the plural.

In the example below, in the phrase **les miens** *(mine)*, the first letter of the possessive pronoun m- refers to the 1st person singular possessor *(mine)*, while the ending **-iens** and the definite article **les** agree with the noun possessed **livres** *(books)* which is masculine plural.

*Where are your books? **Mine** are in the living room.*

Où sont vos livres? **Les miens** sont dans le salon.

1st pers. sing.
possessor

Let us look at the French possessive pronouns to see how they are formed. Since the rules for the selection of a singular possessor are different from the rules for the selection of a plural possessor, we have divided the French possessive pronouns into these two groups:

Singular Possessor: mine, yours (tu **form**), his, hers, its

In French, each of these possessive pronouns has four forms depending on the gender and number of the noun possessed: the masculine singular form, the feminine singular form, the masculine plural form, and the feminine plural form. To choose the proper form follow these steps.

1. Indicate the possessor. This will be shown by the first letter of the possessive pronoun. (They are the same initial letters as the possessive adjectives, see **What is a Possessive Adjective?**, p. 96).

mine	m-
yours	t-
(**tu** form)	
his	
hers }	s-
its	

2. Establish the gender and number of the object possessed. Choose the definite article and the ending according to the gender and number of that noun.

Noun possessed is masculine singular → **le** + first letter of the possessor + **-ien**

*Whose **book** is that?*	*It is **mine**.*
	*It is **yours***
	*It is **his/hers**.*
A qui est ce **livre?**	C'est **le mien**.
noun possessed masc. sing.	C'est **le tien**.
	C'est **le sien**.

Noun possessed is feminine singular → **la** + first letter of the possessor + **-ienne**

*Whose **house** is that?*	*It is **mine**.*
	*It is **yours**.*
	*It is **his/hers**.*
A qui est cette **maison?**	C'est **la mienne**.
noun possessed fem. sing.	C'est **la tienne**.
	C'est **la sienne**.

Noun possessed is masculine plural → **les** + first letter of the posessor + **-iens**

*Whose **books** are those?*	*They are **mine**.*
	*They are **yours**.*
	*They are **his/hers**.*
A qui sont ces **livres?**	Ce sont **les miens**.
noun possessed masc. sing.	Ce sont **les tiens**.
	Ce sont **les siens**.

Noun possessed is feminine plural → **les** + first letter of the possessor + **-iennes**

*Whose **letters** are those?*	*They are **mine**.*
	*They are **yours**.*
	*They are **his/hers**.*
A qui sont ces **lettres?**	Ce sont **les miennes**.
noun possessed	Ce sont **les tiennes**.
	Ce sont **les siennes**.

3. Select the proper form according to the two steps above.

Let us apply these steps to some examples.

> *Mary is looking at her photos. He is looking at **yours.***
> Marie regarde ses photos. Il regarde **les tiennes.**
> 1. Possessor: **t-**
> 2. Noun possessed: **Les photos** *(the photos)* is feminine plural.
> 3. Selection: **les + -iennes**

> *Lend me your book. No, I' ll lend you **hers.***
> Prêtez-moi votre livre. Non, je vous prêterai **le sien.**
> 1. Possessor: **s-**
> 2. Noun possessed: **Le livre** *(the book)* is masculine singular.
> 3. Selection: **le + -ien**

Plural Possessor: ours, yours (vous form), theirs

In French, each of these possessive pronouns has three forms depending on the number of the noun possessed: the masculine singular form, the feminine singular form, and the plural form (the same for both genders). To choose the proper form, follow these steps:

1. Indicate the possessor.

ours	**nôtre**
yours	**vôtre**
theirs	**leur**

2. Establish the gender and number of the noun possessed. Choose the definite article according to the gender and number of the noun possessed.

> noun possessed is masculine singular → **le**
> noun possessed is feminine singular → **la**
> noun possessed is plural → **les** and add an "-s" to the possessor

3. Select the proper form according to the two steps above.

Let us apply these steps to some examples.

> *Whose house is it? It is **ours.***
> A qui est cette maison? C'est **la nôtre.**
> 1. Possessor: **nôtre**
> 2. Noun possessed: **La maison** *(the house)* is feminine singular.
> 3. Selection: **la**

*I will not lend you my cards. I'll lend you **theirs**.*
Je ne vous prêterai pas mes cartes. Je vous prêterai **les leurs.**

1. Possessor: **leur**
2. Noun possessed: **Les cartes** *(cards)* is plural.
3. Selection: **les + - s**

Summary

Here is a chart you can use as a reference.

Possessor		Noun possessed	
Singular		**Singular**	**Plural**
mine	masc.	le mien	les miens
	fem.	la mienne	les miennes
yours	masc.	le tien	les tiens
("**tu**" form)	fem.	la tienne	les tiennes
his, hers, its	masc.	le sien	les siens
	fem.	la sienne	les siennes
ours	masc.	le nôtre	les nôtres
	fem.	la nôtre	
yours	masc.	le vôtre	les vôtres
("**vous**" form)	fem.	la vôtre	
theirs	masc.	le leur	les leurs
	fem.	la leur	

▼▼▼▼▼▼▼▼▼▼▼▼▼▼REVIEW ▼▼▼▼▼▼▼▼▼▼▼▼▼▼▼▼

Underline the possessive pronouns in the sentences below.
- Draw an arrow from the possessive pronoun to its antecedent.
- Circle whether the antecedent is singular (S) or plural (P).
- Using the charts in this section, fill in the French possessive pronoun.

1. I won't take his car. I'll take mine.

ANTECEDENT IN FRENCH: feminine   S   P

Je ne prendrai pas sa voiture. Je prendrai _____.

2. I'm not going with his parents. I'm going with hers.

ANTECEDENT IN FRENCH: masculine   S   P.

Je ne vais pas avec ses parents. Je vais avec _____.

3. Are you taking my book? No, I'm taking yours (familiar).

ANTECEDENT IN FRENCH: masculine   S   P

Prends-tu mon livre? Non, je prends _____

41. WHAT IS A RELATIVE PRONOUN?

A **relative pronoun** is a word that serves two purposes:

1. As a pronoun it stands for a noun or another pronoun previously mentioned. The noun or pronoun referred to is called the **antecedent**.

> This is the boy *who* broke the window.
> |
>   antecedent

2. It introduces a **subordinate clause**, that is, a group of words having a subject and verb, separate from the subject and verb of the main sentence, which does not express a complete thought. A main clause can stand alone as a complete sentence, a subordinate clause cannot.

>   main clause   subordinate clause
> | |
> This is the boy *who broke the window.*
> | |
>   subject verb
> *Who broke the window* is not a complete sentence.

The above subordinate clause is also called a **relative clause** because it starts with a relative pronoun *who*. The relative clause gives us additional information about the antecedent *boy*.

Relative clauses are very common. We use them in our everyday speech without giving much thought to why and how we construct them. The relative pronoun allows us to combine in a single sentence two thoughts which have a common element.

> **sentence a**   I met the teacher.
> **sentence b**   He teaches French in my school.
> **combined**   I met the teacher *who* teaches French in my school.

When sentences are combined with a relative pronoun, the relative pronoun can have different functions in the relative clause. It can be the subject, the direct object, the indirect object or the object of a preposition. Since your selection of the relative pronoun will depend on its function in the relative clause, we shall study each function separately.

IN ENGLISH

In an English sentence, the relative pronoun is often omitted.

The book *that* I'm reading is interesting.
    |
    relative pronoun

The book I'm reading is interesting.
    |_____|_____|
    relative pronoun omitted

The selection of most relative pronouns depends on the function of the relative pronoun in the relative clause, and on whether the antecedent is a "Person" (this category includes human beings and animals) or a "Thing" (this category includes objects and ideas).

IN FRENCH

Relative pronouns are used just as they are in English. The main difference is that, unlike English where the relative pronoun can sometimes be omitted at the beginning of a relative clause, the relative pronoun must always be expressed.

Subject of the Relative Clause

IN ENGLISH

There are three relative pronouns that can be used as subjects of a relative clause, depending on whether the relative pronoun refers to persons or things.

"Person"

Who or *that* is used for the subject of the sentence.

She is the only student *who* answered all the time.
                |
                antecedent
    Who is the subject of *answered.*

She is the only student *that* answered all the time.
                |
                antecedent
    That is the subject of *answered.*

"Thing"
Which or *that* is used for the subject of the sentence.

The movie *which* is playing is in French.
|
antecedent
Which is the subject of *is playing*.

This is the book *that* is so popular.
|
antecedent
That is the subject of *is*.

IN FRENCH
There is one relative pronoun that can be used as subject of a relative clause.

Qui is used as the subject of a relative clause, regardless of whether the antecedent is a person or a thing.

*This is the student **who** answered.*
|
antecedent
Who is the subject of *answered*.
Voici l'étudiant **qui** a répondu.

*This is the book **which** is so interesting.*
|
antecedent
Which is the subject of *is*.
Voici le livre **qui** est si intéressant.

Notice that **qui** is always followed by a verb.

Combining Sentences With a Relative Pronoun Subject

IN ENGLISH
sentence a   The students passed the exam.
sentence b   They studied.

1. Identify the element the two sentences have in common.

The students and *they;* both words refer to the same persons.

2. The relative pronoun always replaces the common element in the second sentence. (Don't forget that a pronoun must refer to something or someone that has already been mentioned.)

> *They* will be replaced by a relative pronoun.
> *(The students* is the antecedent.)

3. The relative pronoun in the relative clause will have the same function as the word it replaces.

> *They* is the subject of studied.
> The relative pronoun will be the subject of *studied.*

4. Choose the relative pronoun according to whether its antecedent is a person or a thing.

> *They* refers to *students.* Therefore, its antecedent is a person.

5. Select the relative pronoun.

> *Who* or *that* is the subject relative pronoun referring to a person.

6. Place the relative pronoun right after its antecedent.

> The students *who* studied passed the exam.
> The students *that* studied passed the exam.
>
> antecedent   relative clause

IN FRENCH

> **sentence a**   Les étudiants ont réussi à l'examen.
> **sentence b**   Ils ont étudié.

Follow the same steps as under In English above, skipping step 4.

> Les étudiants **qui** ont étudié ont réussi à l'examen.
>
> antecedent   relative clause

Direct Object of the Relative Clause

IN ENGLISH

There are three relative pronouns that can be used as direct objects of a relative clause, depending on whether the relative pronoun refers to persons or things. We have indicated relative pronouns in parentheses because they are often omitted.

"Person"
Whom or *that* is used as a direct object of a sentence.

This is the student *(whom)* I saw yesterday.
            |
        antecedent
Whom is the direct object of *saw*.
(I is the subject of the relative clause.)

This is the student *(that)* I saw yesterday.
            |
        antecedent
That is the direct object of *saw*.
(I is the subject of the relative clause.)

"Thing"
Which or *that* is used as a direct object of a sentence.

This is the book *(which)* Paul bought.
          |
      antecedent
Which is the direct object of *bought*.
(Paul is the subject of the relative clause.)

This is the book *(that)* Paul bought.
          |
      antecedent
That is the direct object of *bought*.
(Paul is the subject of the relative clause.)

IN FRENCH
There is only one relative pronoun that can be used as direct object of a relative clause.

Que (or **qu'** before a vowel) is used as the direct object of a relative clause, regardless of whether the antecedent is a person or a thing.

We have included the relative pronouns in the English sentences below to show you what the French relative pronoun relates to; however, since the relative pronoun is often omitted in an English sentence, we have put them between parentheses.

This is the book **(which)** *I bought.*
          |
      antecedent
Which is the direct object of *bought*.
I is the subject of the relative clause.
Voici le livre **que** j'ai acheté.

*This is the student (**whom**) he saw.*
|
antecedent
Whom is the direct object of *saw.*
He is the subject of the relative clause.
Voici l'étudiant **qu'il a vu.**

Notice that **que** is always followed by a noun or pronoun.

Combining Sentences With a Relative Pronoun Direct Object

IN ENGLISH

sentence a   The French teacher is nice.
sentence b   I met him today.

1. Common element: *French teacher* and *him*
2. Element to be replaced: him
3. Function of *him*: direct object
4. Antecedent: *the French teacher* is a person.
5. Selection: *whom* or *that*
6. Placement: *whom* or *that* after *the French teacher*

The French teacher, *whom* I met today, is nice.
The French teacher, *that* I met today, is nice.

antecedent   relative clause

In spoken English, you would say: "The French teacher I met today is nice." Notice that the relative pronoun *whom* or *that* is left out, making it more difficult to identify the two clauses.

IN FRENCH

sentence a   Le professeur de français est gentil.
sentence b   Je l'ai rencontré aujourd'hui.

Follow the same steps as under In English above, skipping step 4.

Le professeur de français que j'ai rencontré aujourd'hui est gentil.

antecedent   relative clause

Indirect Object and Object of a Preposition
in a Relative Clause

Both the relative pronoun as an indirect object and the relative pronoun as an object of a preposition involve prepositions.

It is often difficult to identify the function of a relative pronoun because in English a preposition is often placed at the end of the sentence, separated from the relative pronoun to which it is linked. This separation of a preposition from its object is called a **dangling preposition** (see p. 141).

To make it easier for you to identify a relative pronoun as an indirect object or as an object of a preposition, you will have to change the structure of the sentence so that the preposition is placed before the pronoun. This restructuring will not only make it easier for you to identify the function of the pronoun, but it will also establish the word order for the French sentence.

IN ENGLISH
There are two relative pronouns used as indirect objects, depending on whether you are referring to a person or a thing.

"Person"
Whom is used as an indirect object or as an object of a preposition.

>Here is the student I was speaking *to*.
> |
>   antecedent

This English structure cannot be translated word-for-word into French for two reasons:

1. The French language does not permit dangling prepositions, and

2. The relative pronoun omitted in English must be expressed in French. To establish the French structure, you must restructure the English sentence, placing the preposition within the sentence and adding a relative pronoun. If you are not sure where to place the preposition and the relative pronoun, remember that they follow immediately after the antecedent.

>**Spoken English**   →   **Restructured**
>Here is the student   Here is the student
>I was speaking *to*.   *to whom* I was speaking.

>*Whom* is the indirect object of *was speaking*.

Here is the student I was talking *about*.
         |
    antecedent

As in the case of the indirect object, spoken English often omits the relative pronoun and places the preposition at the end of the sentence. Again, you will have to restructure the sentence.

Spoken English → **Restructured**
Here is the student   Here is the student
I was speaking *about*. *about whom* I was speaking.
    Whom is the object of the preposition *about*.

"Thing"
Which is used as an indirect object or as an object of a preposition.

Here is the museum he gave the painting to.
        |
    antecedent

Spoken English → **Restructured**
Here is the museum   Here is the museum
he gave the painting *to*. *to which* he gave the painting.
    Which is the indirect object of *gave*.

Here is the museum *to which* he gave the painting.
  | |
antecedent   relative clause

IN FRENCH
Relative pronouns used as indirect objects and as objects of a preposition are divided into two main groups discussed separately below: relative pronouns objects of a preposition other than **de** *(of)*, and relative pronouns objects of the preposition **de.** Moreover, the first of these groups is subdivided as to whether the relative pronoun refers to a person or a thing.

Relative pronouns objects of a preposition other than de
This group also covers indirect objects because relative pronouns are objects of the preposition à (see p. 118).

Sometimes there is more than one way to express the relative pronoun in French. We have only given you the most common form and refer you to your French textbook for the others.

"Person"

Preposition + **qui**

*This is the man (**that**) I am thinking about.*
         |
      antecedent

Spoken English →	Restructured
This is the man	This is the man
I am thinking *about.*	*about whom* I am thinking.

Voici l'homme **à qui** je pense.
Remember that *to think about* is **penser à.**

"Thing"

Preposition + **lequel**

Lequel must agree with the antecedent in gender and number. Also, following the preposition **à** *(to)* the initial **le-** and **les-** become **au-** and **aux-.**

*These are the pens (**that**) I write with.*
           |
        antecedent

Spoken English →	Restructured
These are the pens	These are the pens
I write *with.*	*with which* I write.

Voici les stylos **avec lesquels** j'écris.
       | |
    antecedent   masc. pl.

Relative pronouns objects of the preposition de

There is one relative pronoun which is most commonly used after the preposition **de.** We refer you to your French textbook for other less common forms.

"Person or thing"

Dont stands for the preposition **de** and the relative pronoun. It is the most common form.

*This is the man (**that**) I am speaking about.*
         |
      antecedent

Spoken English →	Restructured
This is the man	This is the man
I am speaking *about.*	*about whom* I am speaking.

Voici l'homme **dont** je parle.

Combining Sentences With a Relative Pronoun
Object of a Preposition

IN ENGLISH

> **sentence a**   Mary read the book.
> **sentence b**   I was speaking about it.

> 1. Common element: *the book* and *it*
> 2. Element to be replaced: *it*
> 3. Function of *it:* object of the preposition *about*
> 4. Antecedent: *The book* is a thing.
> 5. Selection: *which*
> 6. Placement: *about which* after *the book*

Mary read the book *about which* I was speaking.

antecedent   relative clause

> In spoken English, you would say: "Mary read the book I was speaking *about.*" Notice that the preposition is at the end and that there is no relative pronoun.

IN FRENCH

> **sentence a**   Marie a lu le livre.
> **sentence b**   Je parlais du livre.

Marie a lu le livre **dont** je parlais.

Possessive Modifier "whose"

IN ENGLISH

The possessive modifier *whose* is a relative pronoun which does not change its form regardless of its function or antecedent.

> Find the woman *whose* car was stolen.
>   antecedent
> *Whose* is a possessive modifying *car.*

> Look at the house *whose* roof burned.
>   antecedent
> *Whose* is a possessive modifying *roof.*

IN FRENCH

The French equivalent of the possessive modifier whose is **dont.**

> *This is the student **whose** mother came.*
> Voici l'étudiant **dont** la mère est venue.

Summary

Here is a chart you can use as reference:

Function in relative clause:	Person	Antecedent	Thing
subject		qui	
direct object		que	
object of **de**		dont	
object of preposition (other than **de**)	prép. + qui		prép. + lequel

To find the correct relative pronoun you must go through the following steps.

1. Find the relative clause. Restructure the English clause if there is a dangling preposition and add the relative pronoun if it has been omitted.

2. Establish the function of the relative pronoun in the French sentence:

   SUBJECT: If the relative pronoun is the subject of the English sentence, it will be the subject of the French sentence → **qui**

   DIRECT OBJECT: If the French verb takes a direct object → **que** or **qu'**

   OBJECT OF THE PREPOSITION DE: If the French verb is followed by the preposition **de** → **dont**

   OBJECT OF A PREPOSITION OTHER THAN DE: If the French verb is followed by a preposition other than **de**?

   ▪ if a person → preposition + **qui**
   ▪ if a thing → preposition + appropriate form of **lequel**

3. Select the French form from the chart above.

Let us apply the steps outlined above to the following sentences:

*The plane **that** comes from Paris is late.*
   1. Relative clause: that comes from Paris
   2. Function of relative pronoun in French: subject of relative clause
   3. Selection: **qui**
L'avion **qui** arrive de Paris est en retard.

*Here are the books (**that**) I bought yesterday.*
1. Relative clause: that I bought yesterday
2. Function of relative pronoun in French: Direct object of **acheter** *(to buy)*
3. Selection: **que**
(Notice the agreement of past participle **achetés** with the direct object **que** referring to **livres** – see p. 64).
Voici les livres **que** j'ai achetés hier.

*Where is the book (**that**) you need?*
1. Relative clause: that you need
2. Function of relative pronoun in French: Object of prepositon **de** *(to need →* **avoir besoin de**) + thing *(book →* **le livre**) masculine singular
3. Selection: **dont**
Où est le livre **dont** vous avez besoin?

*Where is the university (**that**) she is thinking about?*

Spoken English	→	Restructured
Where is the university she is thinking *about?*		Where is the university *about which* she is thinking?

1. Relative clause: about which she is thinking
2. Function of relative pronoun in French: Object of preposition **à** *(to think about →* **penser à**) + thing *(university →* **une université**) feminine singular
3. Selection: **à laquelle**
Où est l'université **à laquelle** elle pense?

*That is the boy (**that**) she is playing with.*

Spoken English	→	Restructured
That is the boy she is playing *with.*		That is the boy *with whom* she is playing.

1. Relative clause: with whom she is playing
2. Function of relative pronoun in French: object of preposition **avec** *(to play with →* **jouer avec**) + person *(boy →* **un garçon**) masculine singular
3. Selection: **qui**
Voici le garçon avec **qui** elle joue.

Relative pronouns are tricky to handle and this handbook provides only a simple outline. Refer to your French textbook for additional rules.

Relative Pronouns Without Antecedents

There are relative pronouns that do not refer to a specific noun or pronoun. Instead they refer to an antecedent which has not been expressed or to a whole idea.

IN ENGLISH

There are two relative pronouns that can be used without an antecedent: *what* and *which.*

What – not referring to any specific noun or pronoun.[1]

> I don't know *what* happened.
> |
>   no antecedent
>   subject

> Here is *what* I read.
> |
>   no antecedent
>   direct object

Which – referring back to a whole idea, not to a specific noun or pronoun.

> You speak many languages, *which* is an asset.
> Antecedent of *which:* the fact that you speak many languages

> She didn't do well, *which* is a pity.
> Antecedent of *which:* the fact that she didn't do well

IN FRENCH

When a relative pronoun does not have a specific antecedent, the pronoun **ce** is added to function as the antecedent. It is followed by whatever relative pronoun would have been used if there had been a noun antecedent.

---

[1]The relative pronoun *what* (meaning *that which*) should not be confused with other uses of *what;* as an interrogative pronoun *(What do you want?* **Qu'est-ce que** vous voulez?, see p. 138), and as an interrogative adjective *(What book do you want?* **Quel** livre voulez-vous?, see p. 101).

Let us apply these rules to the following examples:

*Here is **what** happened.*
Voici **ce qui** est arrivé.
1. Relative clause: what happened
2. Function of relative pronoun in French: subject of relative clause
3. Selection: **qui**
4. No antecedent: add **ce**

*Show me **what** you bought.*
Montrez-moi **ce que** vous avez acheté.
1. Relative clause: what you bought
2. Function of relative pronoun in French: direct object of **acheter** *(to buy)*
3. Selection: **que**
4. No antecedent: add **ce**

*I don't know **what** he is talking about.*
Je ne sais pas **ce dont** il parle.
1. Relative clause: *what* he is talking *about* – Restructured: *about what* he is talking
2. Function of relative pronoun in French: object of preposition **de** *(to speak about →* **parler de)**
3. Selection: **dont**
4. No antecedent: add **ce**

*He doesn't speak French, **which** will be a problem.*
Il ne parle pas français, **ce qui** sera un problème.
1. Relative clause: which will be a problem
2. Function of relative pronoun in French: subject
3. Selection: **qui**
4. No antecedent: add **ce**
(Which refers to the whole phrase "he doesn't speak French.")

*To speak French well, that's **what** I want.*
Bien parler français, voilà **ce que** je veux.
1. Relative clause: what I want
2. Function of relative pronoun in French: direct object of **vouloir** *(to want)*
3. Selection: **que**
4. No antecedent: add **ce**
(What refers to the whole phrase "to speak French well.")

▼▼▼▼▼▼▼▼▼▼▼▼▼▼▼REVIEW ▼▼▼▼▼▼▼▼▼▼▼▼▼▼▼▼▼

Underline the relative pronoun in the sentences below.
- Circle the antecedent.
- Circle the function of the relative pronoun: subject (S), direct object (DO), object of a preposition (OP), object of preposition **de** (OPde), or possessive modifier (PM).
- Using the chart on p. 164, fill the French relative pronoun in the French sentences below.

1. I received the letter that you sent me.

to send → **envoyer**

FUNCTION IN ENGLISH:	S	DO	OP	OPDE	PM
FUNCTION IN FRENCH:	S	DO	OP	OPDE	PM

J'ai reçu la lettre _____ vous m'avez envoyée.

2. That is the young woman who speaks French.

FUNCTION IN ENGLISH:	S	DO	OP	OPDE	PM
FUNCTION IN FRENCH:	S	DO	OP	OPDE	PM

Voici la jeune fille _____ parle français.

3. Here is the man with whom I travelled.

travel with → **voyager avec**

FUNCTION IN ENGLISH:	S	DO	OP	OPDE	PM
FUNCTION IN FRENCH:	S	DO	OP	OPDE	PM

Voici l'homme avec _____ j'ai voyagé.

4. This is the book whose title I had forgotten.

FUNCTION IN ENGLISH:	S	DO	OP	OPDE	PM

Voici le livre _____ j'ai oublié le titre.

5. Paul is the student I spoke of.

Restructure: _____

to speak of → **parler de**

FUNCTION IN ENGLISH:	S	DO	OP	OPDE	PM
FUNCTION IN FRENCH:	S	DO	OP	OPDE	PM

Paul est l'étudiant _____ je parlais.

42. WHAT IS A DEMONSTRATIVE PRONOUN?

A **demonstrative pronoun** is a word that replaces a noun previously mentioned, the antecedent, as if pointing to it. The word *demonstrative* comes from *demonstrate*, to show.

"This one, that one" and "these, those"

IN ENGLISH
The singular demonstrative pronouns are *this (one)* and *that (one)*; the plural forms are *these* and *those*.

> Here are two suitcases. *This one* is big and *that one* is small.
> Choose a book. *These* are in French, *those* in English.

As with the demonstrative adjectives, *this (one)*, *these* refer to a person or an object near the speaker, and *that (one)*, *those* refer to a person or an object away from the speaker.

IN FRENCH
Demonstrative pronouns do not change regardless of their function, but they agree in gender and number with their antecedent. Also, **-ci** is added to indicate objects closer to the speaker and **-là** to indicate objects farther away.

	Singular	Plural
masculine	celui	ceux
feminine	celle	celles

To choose the correct form, follow these steps:

1. Determine the antecedent.
2. Determine the gender and number of the antecedent.
3. Based on steps 1 and 2 choose the correct form from the chart.
4. Add **-ci** for *this* or *these* and **-là** for *that* and *those*.

Look at the following examples.

*Give me the book. **This one.***
Donne-moi le livre. **Celui-ci.**

1. Antecedent: book
2. Gender & number: **Le livre** *(the book)* is masculine singular.
3. Selection: **celui**
4. *This* → **-ci**

Give me the letter. ***That one.***
Donne-moi la lettre. **Celle-là.**
   1. Antecedent: letter
   2. Gender & number: **La lettre** *(the letter)* is feminine singular.
   3. Selection: celle
   4. *That* → **-là**

Give me the books. ***These.***
Donne-moi les livres. **Ceux-ci.**

   1. Antecedent: books
   2. Gender & number: **Les livres** *(the books)* is masculine plural.
   3. Selection: ceux
   4. *These* → **-ci**

Give me the letters. ***Those.***
Donne-moi les lettres. **Celles-là.**
   1. Antecedent: letters
   2. Gender & number: **Les lettres** *(the letters)* is feminine plural.
   3. Selection: **celles**
   4. *Those* → **-là**

"The one, the ones" → celui qui, celui que

The same French demonstrative pronouns (without **-ci** or **-là**) followed by the relative pronoun **qui** or **que** can be used at the beginning of a relative clause. (See **What is a Relative Pronoun?**, p. 154).

IN ENGLISH
The demonstrative pronouns *the one* and *the ones*, unlike *this one* and *that one*, do not point out a specific object, but instead introduce a clause that helps us identify an object by giving additional information about it. There is a singular form *the one* and a plural form *the ones*. They can be followed by the relative pronoun *that* or *which*, but the relative pronoun is often omitted.

   What book are you reading?
   I am reading *the one (that)* I bought yesterday.
      Clause: *the one that I bought yesterday*
      gives us additional information about *the book.*
      Number: *The one* is singular.

   Which dresses do you prefer?
   I prefer *the ones (that)* are in front.
      Clause: *the ones that are in front*
      gives us additional information about *the dresses.*
      Number: *The ones* is plural.

IN FRENCH

The demonstrative pronouns corresponding to *the one* and *the ones* agree in gender and number with the antecedent. The relative pronoun *that* or *which* is selected according to its function in the relative clause (see pp. 164) and must be stated in French.

To choose the correct form, follow these steps:

Demonstrative pronoun *(the one, the ones)*

1. Find the antecedent.
2. Determine the gender and number of the antecedent.
3. Select the correct French form from the chart on p. 169.

Relative pronoun *(that, which—*add it to the English sentence if it has been omitted)

1. Determine the function of the relative pronoun in the relative clause.
2. Select the correct French form:
   ▪ the subject of the relative clause → **qui**
   ▪ the object of the relative clause → **que**

Let us apply these rules to the following examples:

What book are you reading?
*I'm reading **the one (that)** I bought yesterday.*
Quel livre lisez-vous? **Celui que** j'ai acheté hier.
                        masc. sing.   object

Demonstrative pronoun

1. Antecedent: book
2. Gender & number: **Le livre** *(the book)* is masculine singular.
3. Selection: **celui**

Relative pronoun

1. Function: *that* is the object of the relative clause. (Answers the question: "I bought *what* yesterday?" *I* is the subject.)
2. Selection: **que**

Which dresses do you prefer?
*I prefer **the ones (that)** are in front.*
Quelles robes préférez-vous? **Celles qui** sont devant.
                              fem. pl.   subject

Demonstrative pronoun
1. Antecedent: dresses
2. Gender & number: **Les robes** *(the dresses)* is feminine plural.
3. Selection: **celles**

Relative pronoun
1. Function: *that* is the subject of the relative clause. (Answers the question: *"What* is in front?)
2. Selection: **qui**

Celui de **to Show Possession**

The same French demonstrative pronouns (without **-ci** or **là**), followed by the preposition **de** can be used to show possession (see **What is the Possessive?**, p. 18).

For the same reason that "my father's house" can only be expressed in French by the structure "the house of my father," a similar French structure must be used to say the equivalent form "my father's." In this case, the word-for-word English translation of the French structure is "the one of my father." In French, the one agrees in gender and number with its antecedent, here "the house."

To choose the correct form, follow these steps:

1. Find the antecedent of *the one* or *the ones*.
2. Determine the gender and number of the antecedent.
3. Select the form of the demonstrative pronoun (see chart p. 169).
4. Add the preposition **de** *(of)*.

Let us apply these rules to the following examples:

Which house are you selling? ***My father's.***

" the one of my father"

Quelle maison vendez-vous? **Celle de mon père.**

fem. sing.

1. Antecedent: house
2. Gender & number: **La maison** *(the house)* is feminine singular.
3. Selection: **celle**
4. Add **de**

Which books are you reading? ***The young man's.***

"the ones of the young man"

Quels livres lisez-vous? **Ceux du jeune homme.**

masc. pl.

1. Antecedent: books
2. Gender & number: **Les livres** *(the books)* is masculine plural.
3. Selection: **ce**
4. Add **de**

▼▼▼▼▼▼▼▼▼▼▼▼▼▼REVIEW ▼▼▼▼▼▼▼▼▼▼▼▼▼▼▼▼

Circle the the demonstrative pronouns in the sentences below.
- Draw an arrow from the demonstrative pronoun to its antecedent.
- Circle if the antecedent is singular (S) or plural (P).
- Fill in the French demonstrative pronoun in the French sentences.

1. She did not buy my house, because she wants this one.

   ANTECEDENT IN FRENCH: feminine   S   P

   Elle n'a pas acheté ma maison, parce qu' elle veut _____.

2. My courses are more interesting than those.

   ANTECEDENT IN FRENCH: masculine   S   P

   Mes cours sont plus intéressants que _____.

3. What book are you reading? The one I bought today.

   ANTECEDENT IN FRENCH: masculine   S   P

   Quel livre lis-tu? _____ que j'ai acheté aujourd'hui.

ANSWER KEY

1. What is a Noun? 1. boy, classroom, teacher   2. textbook, painting, cover   3. Mary, Evans, Paris, class   4. lion, children   5. truth, fiction   6. kindness, understanding, world

2. What is Meant by Gender? 1. M   2. ?   3. F   4. ?   5. ?   6. F   7. ?

3. What is Meant by Number? The first letter corresponds to Column A, the second to Column B. 1. P P   2. P ?   3. S S   4. S S   5. P P   6. P ?

4. What are Articles? 1. C, les   2. C, l'   3. C, des   4. C, une   5. N, de l'   6. N, le   7. C, un   8. N, de la   9. C, le   10. N, de la

5. What is the Possessive? 1. the parents of some children   2. the color of the dress   3. the entrance of the school   4. the speed of a car   5. the covers of the books

6. What is a Verb? 1. purchase 2. were   3. enjoyed, preferred   4. ate, finished, went   5. was, see, struggle, get out   6. attended, celebrate

7. What is an Infinitive? 1. to do   2. study   3. to learn   4. leave   5. to travel

8. What are Auxiliary Verbs? 1. did   2. will   3. do   4. – *(to have,* **avoir,** is an auxiliary verb in French)

9. What is a Subject? 1. Q: "What rang?" the bell → sing.   Q: "Who ran out?" the children → pl.   2. Q: "Who took the order?" one waiter → sing.   Q: "Who brought the food?" another → sing.   3. Q: "Who voted?" the first-year students (or the students) → pl.   4. Q: "What is a beautiful language?" French → sing.   Q: "What is difficult?" it → sing

10. What is a Pronoun? The antecedent is in parentheses. 1. she (Mary), him (Peter)   2. they (coat, dress)   3. herself (Mary)   4. we (Paul, I)   5. it (bed)

11. What is a Subject Pronoun? 1. je → 1st, sing.   2. vous → 2nd, pl.   3. nous → 1st, pl.   4. tu → 2nd, sing.   5. elles → 3rd, pl.   6. vous → 2nd, pl.   7. ils → 3rd, pl.

12. What is a Verb Conjugation? STEM: port-. CONJUGATION: je porte, tu portes, il (elle) porte, nous portons, vous portez, ils (or elles) portent.

13. What are Affirmative and Negative Sentences? Words that indicate the negative are in italics. Words around which to place **ne...pas** are underlined. 1. We *do not (don't)* want to speak English in class. 2. He *does not (doesn't)* do his homework. 3. Helen was *not* (wasn't) home this morning. 4. Paul cannot (can't) go to the restaurant with us.

14. What are Declarative and Interrogative Sentences? Words that indicate the interrogative are in *italics* I. 1. *Did* Paul and Mary study all evening?   2. *Does* his brother eat a lot?   3. *Do* the girl's parents speak French?   II. 1. *Est-ce que* would precede: my mother and father went to the movies. 2. *N'est-ce pas* would follow: my mother and father went to the movies. 3. noun subject → mother and father; verb → went; pronoun that corresponds to the subject → they → *ils*

17. What is the Present Tense? 1. reads 2. is reading → *lit* 3. does read → *lit*

18. What is the Imperative? I. 1. Study every evening. 2. Let's go to the movies once a week. II. 1. Don't sleep in class. 2. Let's not speak in class. III. 1. P 2. I 3. P 4. I

19. What is a Participle? 1. am speaking 2. were studying 3. are bringing 4. will be trying

20. What is the Past Tense? IMPARFAIT: checked, handled, was crying, was, was leaving PASSÉ COMPOSÉ: went, arrived, ran, dropped, tried, ducked, grabbed, brought, comforted, went

21. What is the Past Perfect Tense? 1. (-1) → P; (-2) → PP 2. (-1) → P; (-2) → PP.

22. What is the Future Tense? 1. ENGLISH: present, future FRENCH: future, future 2. ENGLISH: future, present FRENCH: future, future

23. What is the Future Perfect Tense? 1. (2), (1) 2. (1), (2). In French, the verbs marked (1) take the future perfect; the verbs marked (2) take the future.

24. What is the Conditional? 1. C, I 2. PP, PC 3. I, I 4. F, P

25. What is a Reflexive Verb? 1. themselves → *se* 2. herself → *se* 3. yourself → *te* 4. ourselves → *nous*

26. What is Meant by Active and Passive Voice? 1. cow, cow → Ac, PP 2. bill, parents → Pa, PP 3. bank, bank → Ac, P 4. everyone, everyone → Ac, F 5. spring break, all → Pa, F

29. What is a Descriptive Adjective? The noun or pronoun described is between parentheses. 1. young (man), French (newspaper) 2. pretty (she), long (dress), red (dress) 3. interesting (it) 4. old (piano), good (music) 5. tired (Paul), long (walk)

30. What is a Possessive Adjective? The noun described is between parentheses. 1. my (books), pl. → *mes* 2. your (car), sing. → *ta* 3. our (mother), sing. → *notre* 4. your (clothes), pl. →*vos*

31. What is an Interrogative Adjective? The noun modified is between parentheses. 1. which (courses), pl. → *quels* 2. what (city), sing. → *quelle*

32. What is a Demonstrative Adjective? I. The noun modified is between parentheses. 1. that (restaurant), sing. → *ce* 2. this (test), sing. → *cet* 3. these (houses), pl.→ *ces*

33. What is Meant by Comparison of Adjectives? I. The noun modified is between parentheses. 1. older (teacher) → C+ 2. less intelligent (he)

→ C- 3. as tall as (Mary) → C= 4. the worst (boy) → S 5. better (student) → C

34. What is an Adverb? The word modified is between parentheses. 1. early (arrived) 2. really (quickly), quickly (learned) 3. too (tired) 4. reasonably (secure) 5. well (speaks), very (well)

35. What is a Conjunction? (The words to be circled are in *italics;* the words to be underlined are plain.) 1. Mary *and* Paul, French *or* Spanish. 2. She did not study *because* she was too tired. 3. Not only had he forgotten his ticket, *but* he had forgotten his passport as well.

36. What is a Preposition? 1. about 2. from 3. around 4. contrary to 5. between

37. What are Objects? 1. Q: "The children took what?" a shower → DO. 2. Q: "They ate what?" the meal → DO. Q: "They ate with whom?" their friends → OP. 3. Q: "He sent what?" a present → DO. Q: "He sent a present to whom?" his brother → IO.

38. What is an Object Pronoun? 1. it, DO, DO, book → *le* 2. them, IO, IO, P → *leur* 3. her, OP, OP → *elle* 4. them, OP, OP, no, parents, P → *eux* 5. them, DO, IO, letters, T → *y* 6. them, OP, OP, yes, exams, T → *en*

39. What is an Interrogative Pronoun? 1. who, S, S → *qui* or *qui est-ce qui* 2. who, to whom did you speak, IO, IO → *à qui* 3. what, DO, DO → *que* 4. who, whom are you calling, DO, IO → *à qui*

40. What is a Possessive Pronoun? 1. mine (car), sing. → *la mienne* 2. hers (parents), pl. → *les siens* 3. yours, (book) sing. → *le tien*

41. What is a Relative Pronoun? The antecedent is between parentheses. 1. that (letter), DO → *que* 2. who (woman), S → *qui* 3. whom (man), OP → *qui* 4. whose (book), PM → *dont* 5. Paul is the student of whom I spoke. Paul (student), OPde → *dont*

42. What is a Demonstrative Pronoun? 1. this one (house), sing. → *celle-ci* 2. those (courses), pl. → *ceux-là* 3. the one (book), sing. → *celui*

INDEX